W9-BMM-208

GROWING UP
GOD'S WAY

By
John A. Stormer

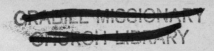
LIBERTY BELL PRESS
P. O. Box 32   Florissant, Missouri

GROWING UP GOD'S WAY
A Liberty Bell Book

ISBN 0-914053-07-8

First Printing, January, 1984
Second Printing, March 1984
Third Printing, June 1984

Liberty Bell Books are published by
LIBERTY BELL PRESS

P.O. Box 32   Florissant, Missouri 63032
Printed in The United States of America

ABOUT THE AUTHOR

Growing Up God's Way is a guide for getting children ready for school and life from birth on. The book is based on John Stormer's experience as a husband and father and his work with hundreds of families during fifteen years as a pastor and Christian school superintendent.

He has been pastor of Calvary Chapel, an independent Baptist church in Florissant, Missouri since 1968. He supervises the education of 300 young people enrolled in kindergarten through grade 12 at Faith Christian School and Academy, a ministry of the church.

He is president of the Missouri Association of Christian Schools and serves on the board of the American Association of Christian Schools. He has preached and lectured in over 35 states and a number of foreign countries.

John Stormer's earlier books, *None Dare Call It Treason* and *The Death of a Nation,* were best sellers in 1964 and 1968. Almost 9-million copies have been sold. Both books dealt with the threat to America's freedom from the growth of world communism and the decay of America's social, political, religious, educational and economic foundations.

He left a successful business career as editor and general manager of an electrical trade magazine in 1962 to devote fulltime to conservative political activities. He was called to preach the Gospel soon after trusting Jesus Christ to be his Savior and Lord in 1965.

A native of Altoona, Pennsylvania, he attended the Pennsylvania State University and graduated from California's San Jose State College in 1954 after Korean War Service as an Air Force historian. He has honorary degrees from Manahath School of Theology (1965) and Shelton College (1976). He and his wife are 30-year residents of Florissant, Missouri, a St. Louis suburb. Their daughter, Holly, is married and is the mother of two small children.

CONTENTS

FOREWORD AND DEDICATION

The job of a writer is similar to that of a physician or a preacher. A doctor's patients usually must hear the bad news before they are willing to undergo the sometimes drastic treatments needed to return them to health. The preacher first shows his congregation the awfulness of sin and the certainty of Hell. This prepares them to receive the Good News that salvation is available as a gift for those who repent and believe that God loves sinners and sent the Lord Jesus to die for them.

The first two chapters of this book document the tragic story of what is happening to children and their parents in America today. The entire book is not filled with bad news, however. Once the "illness" has been described and diagnosed, exciting "remedies" are prescribed. My hope is that what I have written will challenge and help readers to ...

> ... love their children---and then train them so others will love them too.

My first book was dedicated to my daughter Holly with the hope that "her future might be as bright as mine was at age five." The world has not gotten any better in the twenty years since then. However, if this book helps Holly and Steve and a lot of other young parents to learn and apply God's principles for child-rearing, the future of my grandchildren will be even brighter than mine or Holly's was at age five.

My last book called for "a rebirth of the political and spiritual principles" which made America great. That "rebirth" will happen only if a generation of parents build character into their children and train them to "do right."

John A. Stormer
Florissant, Missouri

WILL YOUR BABY BE AMONG THE STATISTICS?

> *Train up a child in the way he should go: and when he is old, he will not depart from it.*
>
> *--Proverbs 22:6*

WHEN BABIES BORN THIS YEAR start to kindergarten in five years, one out of three of them is likely to be labeled "learning disabled." If present trends continue, many others, considered to be "developmentally delayed," will never achieve their full potential.

Will your baby be among them?

A growing number of experts believe that the training, care, love, and discipline you give your baby during the first twelve to thirty-six months will largely determine how well he or she will get along in school and life. According to these experts, what you do now will determine whether your child becomes one of the tragic statistics.

Dr. Burton L. White, longtime director of Harvard University's Preschool Project, has studied thousands of preschool children. They come from varying backgrounds. Based on his studies and research, he's concluded:

The family is the No. 1 influence on the child.

From eight months to three years is the most vital time in a child's life. As a direct result of what parents do---or don't do---lifetime competencies are set. Chances are that the competent child will always be competent. The "slow" child will always lag behind.

Only one child out of ten receives as good a start as he might.[1]

In plain English, Dr. White is saying that most parents do not know how to raise children---or they don't take the time to do the job right. Because most parents fail in some

way nine out of ten children never achieve all they could
accomplish in school and life.

The theories of this Harvard educator concerning the
importance of the child's earliest years have strong Biblical
support. In the Book of Proverbs, God says:

> Train up a child in the way he should go: and when he is old, he
> will not depart from it (Proverbs 22:6).

Failure and frustration are ahead all through life when
babies do not get the right start. By the time this year's
babies enter fourth or fifth grade many of the "learning-
disabled" or "developmentally-delayed" children among
them will be in special education classes. Special programs
for children with academic deficiencies or behavior
problems are the fastest growing area in public education.[2]

A sizable percentage of the "learning-disabled" or
"developmentally-delayed" children who make it to high
school will be "drop-outs." The "learning-disabled" child
who does eventually graduate will probably be among the
growing numbers who receive high school diplomas but are
unable to balance a checkbook or read more than a comic
book. These educated "illiterates" have been given much
publicity by the press, presidential commissions on the
evaluation of education, etc.[3] They are handicapped for
life. The schools are not totally to blame. Often the pattern
of failure starts long before the child comes to school. Such
tragedies do not need to happen.

Children with basic ability who are not making it in
school are much more likely to have other problems as well.
They are among the growing numbers who seek to escape
from their problems with drugs and sex. They often become
bitter and rebellious. They strike out against people and
their property with violence and vandalism. Teenage drug
abuse has increased tenfold in the last twenty years while
pregnancies and venereal disease have increased 400%.[4]
Violence and vandalism have skyrocketed.[5]

Will your baby be "learning disabled" and add to these
tragic statistics? Or will your child go off to school in five
years, fit into the classroom, get along with the teacher and
be basically happy and well adjusted? Will your child learn
to read, count and do at least average work and be a
blessing to you?

What can you start doing right now to keep your baby from growing up to be a learning-disabled child five years from now? The term "learning-disabled" produces a mental picture of children handicapped by eye problems, defective hearing, brain damage or mental retardation. However, only a handful out of every one-hundred "learning disabled children" suffer from real physical handicaps, birth defects, or an IQ which would keep them from functioning in a normal classroom. What then is a "learning-disabled child?"

HISTORY OF THE PROBLEM

In the middle 1960's schools started having problems with growing numbers of incoming kindergartners. The problems were not new, but the increased number of children having the difficulties was noticeable. Veteran teachers mumbled, "Am I getting old---or is every class really getting harder to control and teach?" It was no illusion. Every class did have more children with problems. In many cases they were found to have average or above average intelligence. But in the classroom they manifested many of these symptoms:

> They didn't pay attention. In fact, many didn't seem able to listen. Because they didn't hear instructions, they couldn't follow them. Disciplinary measures, whether withdrawn privileges, spanking, or extra responsibilities had little or no effect. Rewards and incentive systems sparked only a little more response.

> They had little interest in learning to read. Handwriting was usually erratic. With little or no self confidence, they were reluctant to tackle any new task. When they did try they had no perseverance or stick-to-itiveness---they would try briefly and quit. There was no sense of neatness in paperwork, belongings, dress, appearance, etc.

> These children had an inability to play creatively and were often uncoordinated physically.

Emotionally, these learning-disabled children often live in a dream world surrounded by a self-constructed protective shell. Others reach out desperately for someone to cling to. At the same time they are often unable to believe what they are told or trust anyone to fulfill promises. Because they seemingly have never come to accept,

reverence, respect, and love any adult, they are unable to
accept a teacher's love, help, instruction, and discipline.
There is usually little capacity to appreciate anything done
for them. There may be an inability to face or recognize
their own shortcomings, wrongdoings, etc. They may be
unable to tell the truth about little things even when caught
in the act and confronted with the evidence. There may be a
desperate need to find security in possessions to a point
where they take from classmates, teachers, etc.

Depending on the degree of disablement, the learning-
disabled child will have great difficulty functioning in a
normal, disciplined classroom. In extreme cases these
students cannot or will not sit still, listen or concentrate for
more than a minute or so. Severe cases are diagnosed as
"hyperactive" or "hyperkinetic." Drugs are often prescribed to "manage" the problem and calm the children.
The extent of the problem was shown in the late 1960's
when federally-financed projects in test cities such as
Baltimore, Maryland and Omaha, Nebraska placed public
school children with learning difficulties and behavior
problems on medication.[6] In Omaha, nearly 6000 out of
60,000 public school children live on medication prescribed
by their family doctors or a psychiatrist who specializes in
children's problems.

Learning-disabled children with the most severe
problems became part of the fastest growing sector in
public education---the special education classes for behavior
problems and emotionally-disturbed children. For example:

> In St. Louis, Missouri, the St. Louis County Special School
> District started its first program for children considered to be
> "learning-disabled" because of behavior problems and emo-
> tional difficulties in 1965. There were 70 students involved. By
> the 1976-77 school year over 6000 students were enrolled in the
> program![7]

Their more sedate brothers and sisters stayed in regular
classrooms and were passed along from year to year even
though they could not read or function at grade level.
Newspapers started printing stories with headlines like,
"City 8th Graders Slip Again in Basic Skills Test Scores"
and "College Test Scores Lowest Since Mid-50's."[8] By the
middle 1970's almost half of all St. Louis area high school

graduates who entered area colleges had to take remedial courses in English, spelling or reading. As public concern grew, in 1978, Missouri, like many other states, started testing eighth graders to see if they had basic "everyday life survival skills." Statewide, 40% of the first 60,000 students who took the test failed.[9]

The problem was nationwide. Illiterate high school graduates started causing problems for industry as this story from California showed:

> SAN FRANCISCO (UPI) - Four out of every 10 high school graduates are inadequately trained in the "fundamental skills" of reading, writing, and arithmetic, according to the Pacific Telephone Company.
>
> The company's president, Jerome Hull, says 300,000 job applicants are interviewed each year and almost half "will not meet our modest basic requirements."
>
> Most of the interviewees are graduates of public high schools, said Hull, "who have not mastered the most fundamental skills sufficiently to be able to learn even a relatively simple work assignment."

By 1978 high school graduates were not the only ones with problems. In Dallas, Texas the school board decided to test newly hired faculty members. They took the test of basic competency usually given to thirteen-year olds. *Half of them failed!* The teachers were hired anyway---and a three-month attempt to keep the test results a secret followed. Only after Dallas newspapers got an order from the Texas attorney general was the sad story published.[10] Similar situations developed in other states.[11]

If faculty members can't pass---how can they teach students to achieve? Incidentally, students at a private high school in north Dallas did considerably better on the basic competency test than the 535 beginning public school teachers.

To combat these problems, an avalanche of remedial programs poured out of educational publishing houses. Most of it was "ungraded." That meant that textbooks were no longer labeled for grade 4 or 5 or 6 or 7. Instead they were marked "Level D" or E, F, or G. Using these "ungraded materials", a ninth grader could work with fourth-grade material without being embarrassed. His parents were also kept unaware of the lack of progress.

Lots of supplemental materials were developed. In 1977-78, for example, *Scholastic*, the weekly news and feature magazine distributed in schools across America, started publishing a special edition for junior and senior high school students *who read at the second-grade level.*Initial circulation was 50,000 copies!

Many of the new programs were federally financed. Over $10-billion was spent on programs started by the Elementary and Secondary Education Act of 1965. In 1978, a study completed by the prestigious Rand Corporation concluded that the twelve-year, multi-billion dollar federal effort to rescue illiterates was a failure.[12] Educators already knew it and were looking for something better. Stop-gap remedial programs didn't get to the real cause of "learning disablement." The root of the problem was faulty early home training and environment of the child.

"Learning disablement" is the result of serious deficiencies in overall character, personality and skills development.

To function effectively and happily in school and life, a person needs to have certain basic character qualities. Those needed before a child starts to school include attentiveness, obedience, contentment, reverence, faith, patience, truthfulness, meekness, and a sense of being secure. A child who starts to school without these basic traits is seriously handicapped.

Such characteristics do not just happen as children "grow-up". Character must be formed by mom and dad. Children develop the attitudes, values, and mannerisms which make up their personalities from experiences in the home under the influence, example, and training of the parents. It cannot just be "taught." In a very real sense it has to be "caught."

Character and personality are developed first in the home (or should be). Then it is strengthened and reinforced in the church, school, by the boss on the job, etc. As we go on through life other traits are added to the basic list. The process continues through grade school, junior and senior high school, college, and then on the job and in the first years of marriage. Other character traits which need to be developed as we progress in life include diligence, determination, punctuality, thriftiness, dependability, decisiveness, enthusiasm, fairmindedness, flexibility, generosity, and loyalty. Each new trait or set of character qualities prepares us to handle life's next series of experiences and responsibilities.

Children who are deficient in basic character qualities are likely to have difficulty in school. They will also be hindered in developing the additional values and attitudes needed on the job and in marriage, later in life.

On the other hand, a child with even below-average intelligence who is attentive and obedient, who respects his teachers, and who has determination built into his character can achieve in the classroom. Some actually make the honor roll. Any employee with these basic character qualities who is loyal to his employer can be trained to be a lifelong asset to his company.

It became obvious in the early 1970's that crash remedial programs after children start to school were not solving the problems. Therefore, some schools started special testing programs to identify the three and four year olds most likely to be "learning-disabled" when they started to school. "Early childhood education programs" were developed for them. In some areas children were brought to school at three or four years of age. Teachers involved the children in games and other activities to develop attentiveness, listening skills, visual perception, ability to follow instruction, speech patterns, muscle coordination, etc. In other areas teachers were sent into homes. They tried to teach parents how to develop attitudes and skills in their children which would keep them out of the "learning-disabled" category. The programs helped students who already had a basic start in the home. They were of limited long range benefit to children from homes with real problems.

Anyone familiar with the theories of Harvard's preschool expert, Burton White, was not suprised, Dr. White was already on record. He says:

> It's all over by age three. Kids can start to lose their potential after their first birthday, and it's hard to turn them around after three. . .chances are the competent three year old will

always be competent. The "slow" child will likely always lag
behind.[13]

For that reason Dr. White is quoted as saying, "In the
long run, preschool education doesn't amount to a hill of
beans."[14] For this reason, concerned educators have
developed programs to encourage and help parents to give
children a right start from birth on. One of the pioneers was
the Ferguson-Florissant School District in St. Louis county,
Missouri. An innovative program entitled, "Parents As
First Teachers", was developed. In addition to teaching
parents what to expect as a child grows, the literature
outlines experiences and activities parents can expose
children to from birth on. Such public school programs are
limited to the physical and mental needs of children and
cannot deal with spiritual and moral concepts needed for
balanced development.

Some radical educators and government officials have
proposed more drastic solutions. They advocate that the
only way to solve the "learning-disabled" crisis is for the
government to assume almost total responsiblility for a
child's care, training and development soon after birth. As
early as January 1969, *Today's Education*, official journal
of the 500,000-member National Education Association
(NEA), was predicting school in the future for the two-year-
olds including. . .

> . . .the introduction of mandatory foster homes and "boarding
> schools" for children between the age of two and three when
> their home environment was felt to have a malignant
> influence.[15]

The magazine admitted that decisions in the 1970's and
1980's in these areas "could have far-reaching social
consequences" and have "a tinderbox quality." In other
words, the public might explode if it knew what some
educators were considering.

A California congressman introduced HR 2505 on
January 16, 1977, to make their ideas law. It was one of a
series of similar laws proposed in successive sessions of
Congress. Walter Mondale introduced one of the most far
reaching when he was a senator. None have passed *yet*.
Congressman Roybal's bill established the federal frame-
work and funding to provide "a full range of health,

education, and social services" for children up to age fourteen with special emphasis on the care of infants from birth through age five. To be supervised by the Department of Health, Education and Welfare, the law would provide. . .

> . . .a program of daily activities to fully develop each child's potential including preschool, after school, summer, winter, vacation and overnight programs.

The bill authorized constructing a chain of facilities across the country to house the programs and the children involved in them. "Medical, psychological, educational and other appropriate diagnosis" were authorized "with appropriate treatment services including in-home services, and training in the fundamentals of child development for parents. . .and prospective parents."

Services were to be provided initially to "all children who need them" with emphasis on the economically disadvantaged. However, the legislation stated that its ultimate purpose was to. . .

> . . .establish the legislative framework for future expansion of such programs *to provide universally available child-development services.*

Under the bill the government would ultimately have total responsibility for the care and development of all children, and the training of parents. Testifying before a U. S. Senate committee in support of an earlier version of the bill, Dr. Reginald Lourie, President of the Joint Commission on Mental Health of Children, told why "experts" push for total government control of children. Dr. Lourie said:

> There is serious thinking among child researchers that we cannot trust the family alone to prepare young people for the new kind of world---not only are parents unnecessary, but they are too inept to rear their children.[16]

Established, funded, and supervised by the federal government, the program was to be carried out by the states and local governments. While these programs for early childhood education and development were being studied at the national level, states were considering bills which fit into the same pattern.

In Missouri, for example, HB 901 was introduced in 1978

to establish machinery within the department of elementary and secondary education to coordinate all "early childhood education and child development services" for children "from birth to age six." The new agency was to have responsibility for "screening and diagnostic services . . .educational programs for preschool children. . .related parent education. . .health and mental health services . . .social services and child care services." Authorization was included for the new agency. . .

> . . .to apply for, receive and administer federal funds not designated to other specific agencies, which are, or may become available under federal programs pertaining to early childhood education and development.

The bill would have established a channel in Missouri for implementing revolutionary federal early childhood education and development programs like those in HR 2505. The Missouri bill had seventy-one co-sponsors. It was supported by the governor, the state commissioner of education, the Missouri affiliates of the National Education Association, teachers' unions, local school superintendents, and some parent groups. Many supporters did not recognize how the legislation fit into a blueprint for ultimately changing the whole structure of family life and child care and training. When concerns were raised, the bill was defeated by a narrow margin---at least for the 1978 legislative session.

A REAL NEED

Supporters of programs for early childhood education and development are concerned about very real needs. Too many families are failing to give children the right start in life. By 1983, experts testifying for legislation for early childhood testing and training claimed that nearly 80% of all children are being handicapped---many of them for life---because they have not had proper character training and development.

As serious as the problem is, should government and the schools get into the child raising and training business? Can they even do the job when parents do fail?

Instead of giving children to the government, can families be brought to see how failure to fulfill their responsibilities affects the future of their children so tragically? Once parents have been challenged, can they be taught how to "train up a child in the way he should go?"

For at least 6000 years families have done the job. Most have done it well. Some have failed. The great men and women of history---George Washington, Abraham Lincoln, John Wesley, Clara Barton---were all products of the training they received in loving, disciplined homes.

Can today's children escape "learning disablement" and become well-adjusted, happy, productive citizens? They will only if individual parents make the commitment to "train up their children in the way they should go." Are *you* willing to make the effort? Are *you* willing to be helped to be the mom or dad God means you to be? It is *your* choice.

Actually, the choice is not one of just keeping your children from being "learning disabled." For twenty years, juvenile crime rates have spiraled higher year after year. Widespread drug use, violence and vandalism in the schools, a tripling of teenage suicides, and a 500% increase in teenage pregnancies all indicate that something is lacking in the way we are raising our children. Behind all of the statistics and ruined lives are little children who did not have their character properly formed and developed. The homes and family must accept the responsibility for the failures. The Bible makes it plain that behavior in life is the result of childhood training---or lack of it. Proverbs 22:6 says:

> Train up a child in the way he should go: and when he is old, he will not depart from it.

What has happened? How has it all come about? Have the ways children are trained changed so drastically in the last 20 years so as to produce these tragic results? Let's look at the record.

Chapter I

1. St. Louis *Globe Democrat*, Mar 4-5 and Sep 29, 1978
2. See page 4
3. Report of Presidential Commission, 1983.
4. See pages 14-15
5. See page 14
6. *This Week* Magazine, Feb 9, 1969

7. Report: The Special School District of St. Louis County, League of Women Voters of Metropolitan St. Louis, 1978, pg. 7
8. St. Louis *Globe Democrat*, Sep 8, 1975, June 16, 1978
9. St. Louis *Post Dispatch*, Sep 24, 1978
10. *Human Events*, Jan 13, 1979
11. St. Louis *Globe Democrat*, Mar 6, 1979
12. St. Louis *Post Dispatch*, Aug 30, 1978
13. St. Louis *Globe Democrat*, Mar 4-5, 1978
14. Ibid., Sep 29, 1978
15. *Today's Education,* Journal of the National Education Association, Jan 1969, pg. 30
16. Indianapolis *News*, Jul 12, 1972
17. Hearing on HB 143, Committee on Elementary and Secondary Education, Missouri House of Representatives, 1983

Chapter II

THE REVOLUTION WE'VE
LIVED THROUGH

*Thou shalt keep therefore his statutes, and his command-
ments which I command thee this day, that it may go well
with thee, and with thy children after thee.*

--Deuteronomy 4:40

THE TYPICAL "learning-disabled child" of the last
dozen years is the product of a subtle revolution in the
American way of life. So are the troubled juvenile
delinquents, the violent and the vandals, and those using
drugs to escape from responsibility or the hurts of growing
up. The young who get into trouble sexually while
desperately reaching out for security and someone to cling
to are other casualties of "The Revolution We've Lived
Through."

New life styles and new attitudes toward life in the years
since 1960 have visibly changed the total environment into
which many children are born and grow up. Learning-
disabled children are not the only symptom that we have
lived through a revolution. Every area of our lives, our
government, and our culture have been touched. Comparing
America in 1960 with today shows how great the changes
have been.

In 1960 there were no X-rated or R-rated movies, or four-
letter words on radio and TV. There were no bars with
"topless" waitresses and no sexual supermarkets operating
openly as "massage parlors." There was no "gay rights"
movement. Homosexuals were called "queers" and hid
their sin rather than proudly parading it before a
complacent world. Most women were women and looked
and acted like it. Men were glad and acted like men. Rock

music was just starting to become popular. There was no teenage drug problem or long-haired hippies. Tranquilizers weren't the #1 selling prescription drug. Birth-control pills were just being introduced. Because abortions were illegal, 1¼-million babies were not being murdered in their mothers' wombs every year.

Prayer and Bible reading were permitted in public school classrooms. That armed security guards were not needed then to prevent violence and vandalism in school hallways was probably not a coincidence. Travelers could get on airplanes in major airports without having their baggage searched or X-rayed to prevent hijackings. A visitor to a major city could safely leave the hotel for a leisurely evening walk through downtown streets without fear of being mugged, robbed, or raped.

It had been almost sixty years since a president or other major figure had been assassinated. Rioters had never burned the center of a major city. No president or vice-president of the United States had ever left office in disgrace rather than face impeachment and a possible jail term.

IT'S DIFFERENT NOW

Things have changed a lot since 1960. The host of learning disabled children is just one symptom. Crimes against people—rape, assault, and murder—have increased 400%.[1] Child abuse, wife beating, and "granny bashing" have all skyrocketed.[2] Over 70,000 teachers are assaulted by students in their classrooms every year.[3] Repair of vandalism costs schools $600-million yearly.[4] The number of teenagers using drugs and alcohol—or who have experimented with them—has mounted year by year.[5]

Divorce is up 60% since 1960 and one out of two marriages now break up.[6] Sixty percent of all married women work outside the home including one out of two mothers with preschool children.[7] Many, many fathers hold two jobs. In some major cities one out of two babies is illegitimate.[8] Nationally one out of six babies is born out of wedlock—about three times the rate of illegitimate births in 1960. A government study shows that 42% of women under twenty have been married less than eight months when their first child is born.[9] Another agency—the Census Bureau—

reported that the numbers of men and women living together without being married doubled between 1970 and 1977.[10]

It is all part of the revolution that we have lived through. Actually, this "revolution" in life styles has been developing for several generations. It has touched every area of American life and culture. It has drastically changed how children are raised.

That it has happened since 1960 was demonstrated by two big power blackouts which darkened New York City. The first was in 1965. The other came twelve years later. Both affected basically the same areas and involved the same segments of the population. What happened during the blackouts though was dramatically different. In 1965 when the lights went out in New York, a few stores were broken into. There were a few isolated instances of looting. It was far different when the power went off in 1977. The United Press reported:[11]

> An army of night stalkers preyed on the blacked out neighborhoods of the city through the night of the power failure. An orgy of looting resulted in more than 3000 arrests and about 900 fires—55 of which were considered major blazes—at a cost of billions to small businessmen.

> Insurers said claims could run as high as a billion dollars but many of the ravaged businesses had no insurance and could file no claims for losses. Officials said 3000 persons had been arrested for looting, possession of stolen property and vandalism. *In contrast during the Northeast power blackout in 1965 fewer than 100 persons were arrested.*

> 'In 1965 you were dealing with human beings,' said a detective assigned to the blighted Bedford-Stuyvestant section during the blackout. 'Now you are dealing with animals. This is an absolute disgrace.'

These changes in America have taken place in less than fifteen years. They are all part of the revolution we've lived through.

WHAT HAS HAPPENED?

What has caused these drastic changes in our society? What is causing crime and corruption, violence and vandalism, drug abuse, changing moral standards and the selfishness which destroys marriages? If the Bible is true—

and it is---the revolution we have lived through has resulted from changes in the way we are raising our children. The Bible says if we train up a child in the way he should go that he will not depart from it when he is old. Because people are behaving differently today the logical conclusion must be that there have been some important changes in the way we train children.

In the introduction to the revision of his best-selling book, *Baby and Child Care*, Dr. Benjamin Spock tells why child-training methods have changed over the last several generations. He writes:

> The rearing of children is more and more puzzling for parents in the twentieth century because we've lost a lot of our old fashioned convictions about what kind of morals and ambitions and characters we want them to have. We've even lost our convictions about the purpose of human existence.[12]

Dr. Spock puts his finger on the problem. If mom and dad have no specific clearcut ideas of what they want their child to become, they will have a difficult or impossible time devising a program to develop the desired characteristics in the child. The child will just grow up to do "his own thing." How about you? Do you really know specifically what kind of morals and convictions and character you want your child to have? Do you know how to start training your baby *now* to develop these characteristics? Or---has "the revolution we've lived through" so influenced you that your baby will just grow up"to do that which is right in his own eyes?"

If you are not aware that a revolution has so drastically changed our society and the way we raise our children, you are typical of so many young parents. Dr. Spock explains why when he says:

> You may not be conscious of these changes---because you are so much a part of these times.[13]

A LOOK AT THE PAST

Down through the ages most people have raised their children the way they were trained themselves. Most new parents just assumed that the way they had been trained was the way to do it. When they weren't sure about some detail they looked to their parents or grandparents for guidance. The child-raising advice and help they were given had usually been passed down through the ages. It came, not from child psychologists or other "professionals", but from our Judeo-Christian heritage and the Bible.

God made man. The Bible is God's instruction manual for life. It tells man how to live, govern himself, manage his affairs, train his children, etc. It also tells sinful man how to be reconciled to a holy God. The Bible with its message has the power to change lives. It gives individuals the desire and ability to live for others. Until the last two or three generations, almost all Americans were reared using Biblical principles---whether they knew it or not. The virtues that are the foundation of stable families and stable societies---obedience, respect for authority, truthfulness, thrift, diligence, hard work, punctuality, dependability--- are all Bible based.

Three things have happened to break the cycle of rather successful child-raising which has gone on for centuries. They are:

> People move more today and are rearing children away from their hometowns and access to the advice and guidance and supervision of parents and grandparents.

> Over a period of several generations, major church denominations moved away from interpreting the Bible literally. Society, therefore, started looking to "experts" and their new theories and ideas for answers to life's problems. In the process, the time-tested methods and truths that have worked for raising children, keeping marriages together, etc., down through the ages have been lost.

> As the new child raising theories have failed, parent-child relationships have deteriorated. As a result there is a new generation of children today who would not ask for advice from mom or dad about anything---and particularly about raising children.

HOW HAS IT HAPPENED?

In the late 1940's a generation which had gone off to war and come back to college or a job started to raise families. A bigger percentage than ever before settled down somewhere away from their hometowns. They were away from their families, their friends, their churches, and all other stabilizing influences. When they needed help in raising their children, they looked not to parents or grandparents but to a book.

The book was Dr. Benjamin Spock's *Baby and Child Care*. It was published in 1945. Nearly one million copies were sold the first year. Since then about thirty-million have come off the press and gone into the hands of anxious young people. Except for the Bible, it is the biggest seller of this century. The book combined a lot of simple medical advice parents wanted with a rather permissive, do-your-own-thing philosophy of child raising. Millions of babies were raised on Dr. Spock in the 1940's, 1950's, and 1960's. They are now raising their own children—and grand-children—and they don't know how to do it.

Actually, it is not all Dr. Spock's fault. His book, which has been the "bible" on child care for thirty years, was issued in 1945. The nation had just come through a depression and a war. Millions of GI's came home from war and they had had enough strict discipline. They were ready to relax. Their churches, for the most part, had already moved away from using the Bible as an absolute standard for life. It was an era when absolutes were not popular. The "experts" in every field were teaching that things can't be "black or white" but just "shades of gray."

The nation was ready for an "expert" who not only permitted but recommended an easy-going, do-your-own-thing type of child raising. The nation was indeed looking for someone who would teach them that schedules were not important and that babies do best if they are fed whenever they want to eat. America was ready for an expert who would assure them that. . .

> Parents who incline to an easy-going kind of management, who are satisfied with casual manners as long as the child's attitude is friendly, or who happen not to be particularly strict—for instance, about promptness or neatness—can also raise children who are considerate and cooperative as long as the parents are not afraid to be firm about those matters that do seem important to them.[15]

The nation was ready for Dr. Spock. In fact, if he had not appeared, the country would probably have invented him. The difficulty is that a nation which is told that it is OK to be easygoing on some things will usually find it impossible to be firm in anything---and that is what has happened. Parents who followed Spock's easygoing child-raising methods produced the hippie generation.

The failure of new child raising methods since World War II has had a drastic effect on parent/child relationships. Dr. Jack Hyles, pastor of the giant First Baptist Church of Hammond, Indiana, has worked with thousands of teenagers. He estimates that 85% of them do not have a good relationship with their parents. Dr. Spock tells why. He says:

> If your upbringing was fairly strict in regard to obedience, manners, sex, truthfulness, it's natural, almost inevitable, that you will feel strongly underneath, about such matters when raising your own children.[16]

Spock confirms here that if you "train up a child in the way that he should go, when he is old, he will not depart from it." He goes on to describe the conflict which develops when a parent, in rearing his own children does turn away from his upbringing and follows the advice of permissive, do-your-own-thing child-raising experts. He says:

> You may have changed your theories because of what you've studied or read or heard, but when your child does something that would have been considered bad in your childhood, you'll probably find yourself becoming more tense, or anxious or angry than you imagined possible.[17]

The parent who still has some convictions (although they may not be very strong) cannot comprehend why his child has none. Parents are dismayed when children have not turned out to be obedient, neat, truthful, punctual, mannerly, etc. even though on the advice of "experts" they did not train these characteristics into them. The parent becomes more and more frustrated. As the frustration mounts, a real gulf develops between the child and the parent. As the problem becomes more widespread, newspapers and magazines start printing stories, as they did in the early 1960's, about a "generation gap." As the gap widens embittered children who had little or no communication with their parents start escaping from the hurts with rock music, drugs, sex or running away. At its heart the "generation gap" is really a "training gap." One generation was trained to have certain standards, values, morals, habits, etc. These values were not passed along to their children. Then the parents could not understand why the younger generation thought and acted differently than they did. Their frustration, disgust or dismay widened the gap and made it deeper.

Actually, it took more than one generation to bring America to where one out of three children is in serious difficulty in school and life. Dr. Spock tells why:

> The reason that most parents have been able to do a good job with their children during the past fifty years of changing theory is that they themselves had been brought up reasonably happily, were comfortable about raising children the same way, and didn't follow any new theory *to extremes.*[18]

However, each generation has accepted more and more permissiveness. Now as the child raising experts' theories of "let the child do his own thing---be a buddy with your child---treat him as an equal" have filtered down to the third generation, a disaster is in the making. The cumulative effect of permissive philosophies and the resultant changed life styles have drastically affected parental influence on the character development of today's children in three ways:

   ---the time most parents spend with children from birth until they start to school and after has been sharply reduced.

   ---even when parents have the time, their ability and know-how and often their desire to shape and influence their children's lives and character have changed.

   ---because parental influence and guidance has lessened, the TV, ideas of friends, etc. are filling the vacuum.

It takes time to train children "in the way they should go." Today's parents are not investing their time to shape their children's lives and character. The results can be tragic.

Chapter II

1. Chicago *Daily News*, Sep 3, 1976
2. St. Louis *Globe Democrat*, Feb 21, 1978, York, Pa Times, Jan 30, 1978
3. St. Louis *Globe Democrat*, Apr 10, 1975
4. Ibid., Sunday Magazine, Dec 4, 1977

5. New York *Times*, Jul 15, 1969; St. Louis *Post Dispatch*, Sep 29, 1974
6. St. Louis *Globe Democrat*, Nov 29-30, 1975; Apr 21, 1980
7. *U.S. News and World Report*, Oct 27, 1975
8. St. Louis *Globe Democrat*, Jul 30-31, 1977
9. St. Louis *Post Dispatch*, Apr 8, 1970
10. St. Louis *Globe Democrat*, Apr 17, 1978
11. St. Louis *Post Dispatch*, Jul 5, 1977
12. Spock, *Baby and Child Care*, 4th Edition, Simon and Schuster division of Gulf & Western Corporation, Copyright 1976, pg 11
13. Ibid.
14. Chicago *Sun Times*, Jan 23, 1974
15. Spock, *Baby and Child Care*, pg. 10-11
16. Ibid.
17. Ibid.
18. Ibid.

Chapter III

RAISING CHILDREN
TAKES TIME

*The rod and reproof give wisdom: but a child left to himself
bringeth his mother to shame.*

--Proverbs 29:15

WHEN NEW KINDERGARTEN CLASSES start to
school each fall, more and more children show evidence
that insufficient time has been invested in their training
and development. They do not know how to listen, obey, or
do simple tasks for themselves. They have not been trained
in manners, respect or concepts of neatness. They have just
grown up.

Because teaching and training time is also "loving time",
many are hungry for love. Some have had so very little love
that they do not know what love really is or how to accept it
from a teacher or classmate.

Many of the children come from one-parent homes where
the mother must work. Rapidly rising divorce rates, particularly among young marrieds, is one result of the
"revolution" in the American way of life. There are also
more unmarried mothers now. More of them choose to keep
their babies. As a result, each new kindergarten class has
more children who have spent most of their waking hours
with a babysitter.

Having a "substitute mother" take over early in life is not
limited to one-parent homes. Young marrieds who want the
life style they believe can be produced by two incomes often
send the mother back to work soon after baby's birth.
Today 60% of all married women work outside the home---
including many young mothers. An estimated 25-million
children live in homes where the mother works. It is all part
of "the revolution in the way we live."

After eight hours on the job, the working mother comes home tired and tense. Even so, she cannot relax. The awesome responsibilities of being wife, mother and home-maker still need to be faced. Few women can handle the two full-time jobs adequately. The child who has grown up in such an atmosphere is usually a different type of person than the baby who develops in a traditional home situation.

All children handicapped by character deficiencies do not come from homes with working mothers, as we shall see. And, although a full-time mother is best, a broken home and a working mother does not doom a child to a certain future as a "learning-disabled" statistic. To do the job, however, the parent needs the desire and determination to learn how to develop a child's character. Then the plan must be followed day after day, month after month, and year after year.

To make this type of commitment, parents need to recognize the pitfalls of not spending enough time with their children---and not wisely using what time is available.

TIME TO TALK

Parents who are away from home all day cannot spend the hours a full-time mother does (or should) with her children constantly. . .

> . . .talking, teaching, playing, providing, inspiring, encouraging, disciplining, observing, reassuring, reading and answering all the "why's." There aren't the hours to do the 1001 "little things" again and again and again which ultimately shape a child's habits, interests, desires, ability, and personality. Most of all, the love a mother shows (or should show) during all these hours through her voice, her touch, her concern, and her presence gives the baby the security and sense of self-importance and belonging which is vitally important to developing as a happy, well-balanced person.

None of these activities---talking, playing, teaching, reading, inspiring, etc.---can be neglected without marring the child's development in some way. For example: A mother who cares for her own baby, talks to the child (or should) hour after hour---often without realizing it. She talks as she feeds, as she changes, as she works in the home. She sings as she settles the baby for a nap. She talks as she plays. When the baby cries, the mother asks,

"What's wrong, honey?" She soothes and comforts.

Even before the baby fully understands what the mother is saying, her voice conveys assurance, interest, concern and love. The baby learns to discern changing attitudes toward himself from the tone of voice. As the months go by, he begins to understand more fully what is being communicated. He comes to realize the importance of the spoken word and begins to apply it to himself personally. He is also accumulating bits and pieces of information about life and the world around him.

Babies and small children who grow up in an impersonal environment where they are not consistently talked to directly and personally do not learn these vital lessons. They do not learn to listen. They may even construct a wall around themselves. Behind this wall they build a dream world in which to live. Unless they become accustomed to getting pleasure and information by being talked to, they have no reason to listen. When such children come to school the teacher has a real problem. Because students have not learned to listen, they do not hear instructions and directions. If they have not heard, they cannot obey and they cannot learn. Extreme cases are, in a sense psychologically deaf. How it can happen is illustrated by this sad but true story:

> My wife and I were married almost eight years before our daughter was born. Until then, Buff, our cocker spaniel, got much of the attention a child normally receives. When I came through the door, I greeted her and she jumped all over me. I played with her. When I had a snack to "hold me over" until dinner, we shared it. If I found some leftovers in the refrigerator at bedtime, Buff and I both ate.
>
> Then suddenly the combination of a new baby, increased responsibilities on my job and deep involvement in political and educational projects in the community took all of my time and interest. When I was home I played with the baby, talked to my wife, and sang to the baby. When I came into the house I was often too preoccupied with pressing responsibilities to pay attention to the dog or even greet her.

Several years passed. The dog got fed, walked, and cared for. Her physical needs were met---sometimes grudgingly. She aged noticeably. She no longer came jumping when I came through the door. When I did try to call her, she did not respond even though I was just a few feet from her. She just did not seem to hear. We attributed the apparent loss of hearing and loss of interest to aging. But then we noticed that she seemed to respond to some noises---some sounds.

> It appeared that if I got her attention and stimulated her, she could hear just as she always did. It finally became obvious that Buff was not actually deaf. We had just gotten too busy to talk with her, play with her, and love her. She quit listening because she no longer expected to be talked to. It was a sad day when we realized how we had gotten so preoccupied that we so sadly neglected our little dog.

Tragically, the same thing is happening to thousands of children today. When they get to school they are among those classified as "learning-disabled." Actually, they have just never learned to listen because no one has talked to them.

Not being talked to affects the ability to listen *and* the ability to talk as well. Vocabulary, confidence in voicing feelings and opinions, and answering questions in school all suffer when children are not talked to consistently and personally and directly.

THE TV IS NO SUBSTITUTE

A good part of this generation of children has grown up with the TV. It is the principal babysitter, companion, instructor, and parent. Children start watching TV as soon as they can sit up. Studies indicate they may watch as much as 4000 hours before starting school and 18,000 by the time they graduate---if they do.

The TV may keep a child occupied, but it is not an adequate substitute for continually being talked to by a loving parent. It does not build the needed kind of attentiveness, listening ability, and word knowledge needed to function later in school and life. The TV, for example, never stops and asks, "Did you understand what I just said?" The TV does not encourage---or permit---two-way communication.

The child can't stop the TV to ask, "Why?" When he misunderstands, he may not even realize it. He lives in a dream world where he has to figure out everything for himself. Eventually he just accepts an existence in an impersonal world of pictures and sounds where he does not

expect to understand certain things. He is on his way to
being a learning-disabled statistic.

TAKE TIME TO READ

Experienced teachers note a definite correlation between
the amount of time parents spend reading to a child and his
own desire to learn to read. Reading is a key to success in
school. All other subjects are dependent upon reading
skills. A reading disability will handicap a person all
through life. An important factor in whether a child learns
to read or not---and how well he will ever read---is his desire.
Parents build this desire by reading to small children.

The child who is regularly cuddled in a parent's arms and
read to---even before he may understand---comes to associate
books with pleasure and being loved. As children grow a
little older, the printed page is the doorway to information,
adventure, excitement, and all sorts of new friends. As
early as the third year the child will "read" the stories
which have become familiar from being read aloud again
and again. By age four, the child will start to manifest a
real desire to learn to himself. He is prepared in this key
area and ready for school.

Reading to a child takes time, but it is vitally important.
It creates a desire in the child to learn to read. It also plays a
part in introducing the child to the world. Gladys Hunt, in
her excellent book, *Honey For A Child's Heart,*[1] writes:

> What fun it is to encourage a personal awareness of words in a
> child---the delight of sound, the color and variety of words
> available to our use. I am not suggesting vocabulary drills
> which teach by rote the meaning of large words. That is quite
> different than feeling the beauty of words. Books, the right
> kind of books, can give us the experience of words. They have
> power to evoke emotion, a sense of spiritual conviction, an
> inner expansion that fills a child to the brim so that 'the years
> ahead will never run dry.'

Reading to children does more than just build a desire to
read and create an awareness of words and the world
around us. It is also an important character-building tool.
Mrs. Hunt writes:

> Good literature teaches more than we know. Example always
> speaks louder than precept, and books can do more to inspire
> honor and tenacity of purpose than all the scoldings and

exhortations in the world. . .The best teaching we have done in our family has been through reading the Bible and good books aloud together. It is not really such a profound concept. How would you best be enlightened to some truth—by being told that it was wrong to be nasty and thoughtless to others, or to meet and come to love some character in a story and then feel her hurts when someone is unkind and says cruel things?

Reading aloud to children helps build good character traits. It also gives children a look into the lives of those who will become their heroes.

Reading time is also "getting to know each other" time. There are millions of heartbroken parents across America today who realized too late that they never got to "know" their children. When a teen-ager turns to drugs, gets pregnant out of wedlock, runs away from home, gets arrested, or commits suicide, the sad realization comes, "I don't really know her." The question then comes, "Why didn't she talk to me about the problem?" It is usually too late then to start. Gladys Hunt writes:

> You can't one day decide to know your children and have it happen. You begin from the beginning. . .knowing someone means sharing ideas, growing together. It means not being embarrassed about feelings or yourself. . .You can't wait to begin when they are grown up. You begin talking and sharing and listening when they are little.

As a family reads together, there are opportunities to talk about the feelings and attitudes of the characters. The next step of sharing our own feelings, desires, wants, etc. comes very naturally. Laurence Housman in his book, *The Unexpected Years*, tells how reading helped his family. He wrote:

> . . .family readings formed so satisfying a bond between older and younger that I can hardly think of family life without it; and I marvel when I hear of families in whose upbringing it had no place.

Today, millions of children are not read to. Parents do not have the time. Some do not see the need. Many hate to read because they never really learned to read themselves. And—in many, many families the TV is a crippling substitute for reading, for conversation, for fun and for getting to know one another.

TV can effectively kill a child's desire to learn to read---or dull his determination enough so that he will not stick to it when the going gets tough.

God places within every child a fantastic desire to know. That is why they start asking thousands of "why's" about everything as soon as they can talk. This hunger is satisfied when children have opportunity for conversation and particularly when they are read to. As they grow, children develop a desire to "feed" themselves from books. It is similar to the way they grow into a desire to feed themselves from the plate. They use their fingers first and then, if guided, they use a fork and spoon.

The TV, however, satisfies the hunger to know without depending on the parents' willingness to read. The TV also satisfies the hunger without requiring the concentration and diligence needed to learn to read---so why bother? The dulled desire which results is a major factor in "Why Johnny Can't Read."

IT TAKES TIME TO TEACH

Conscientious, hard working mothers develop shortcuts to improve their efficiency and save time and effort. Some efficiency steps can be helpful. Others can shortchange the child in the longrun. For example:

> It may be easier and quicker for a mother to do the family's shopping on the way home from work *before* picking up her child at the babysitter. However, the child then misses the magic of the store with all its opportunities to learn and experience. Learning to walk at mother's side, identifying and picking up the cans and other items mother asks for in each aisle, all expand vocabulary, skills, and awareness which will be used later in life.

When children get older, shopping can continue to be a time of parent-child fellowship. Of course, the level of teaching is increased. Relative prices of small sizes vs. large ones and the merits of name brands vs. private labels, can be discussed. Every situation in life provides teaching opportunities and they all take time. Another example is...

> ...it's lots quicker to dress a child yourself when rushing to get to the babysitter and then to work or an appointment than to try to teach a small child how to dress himself. However, the cost in undeveloped skill; and the loss of the thrill and self-

confidence which comes to a child when he learns each new step in dressing himself cannot be measured in saved minutes.

With Sunday the only free day to sleep late or to catch up on chores, modern parents often feel that church is a luxury they cannot work in. However. . . .

> . . .a child needs the example of Godly parents to develop his own reverence and respect for God. He needs the experience of meeting with others as a family. He needs the discipline of learning to sit still and listen at a very early age. Even a two-year-old needs the thrill of being "promoted" from the nursery into a "real" class.

Bible-believing churches have nurseries for newborn infants. Sunday school classes are offered for two-year-olds. They have special toddlers' and children's church services as well.

There are 1001 "little things" to teach a child. They all take time. They are all important to the child's immediate development and to how the child will succeed in school and later in life. Each "little thing" takes time. Yet they are all important. For example. . .

> . . .it takes time *and* persistence *and* patience to teach a small child how to hold and use a knife, fork and spoon properly.

Is it worth the effort? What is really important about your child accepting and following your instructions on the correct way to use a fork? There are at least three important long-range benefits from making an effort in this seemingly insignificant little area. They are: (1) When your child starts using the fork as you require, he has made a decision which will help him in a year or so. He is being prepared to submit to the teacher who wants him to hold a pencil in a certain way. (2) It will help make him to be "teachable" on the job later in life. (3) Knowing how to eat right will give him more confidence in social situations throughout life. The immediate benefits are: (1) The contacts you have with your child while you are teaching him; (2) the sense of accomplishment he will get when he is able to do what you have asked; and (3) the praise he will enjoy from you as a reward for obedience.

IT TAKES MORE TIME TO TRAIN

It takes time to *teach* children the multitude of things

they need to know. It takes even more time to *train* them to
do consistently what they have been taught.

Teaching without training produces tragedy.

A generation of heartbroken parents, frustrated teachers,
and sincere but misguided social workers need to learn the
difference between teaching children—and training them.

Teaching instructs a child in what is right and wrong.
Teaching spells out what is acceptable behavior and what
is not. *Training* combines such teaching with requiring the
child to always do what he has been taught. Training
involves applying penalties whenever he does wrong. This
takes so much time.

Teaching without training really tells the child, "What I
am teaching you is not really important because if it were, I
would require you to do it." Teaching without training is
hypocrisy. Teaching without training results in sullen,
mixed up, insecure, rebellious young people. They will grow
up to be misfits in a world which demands responsible
actions. Children who have been taught but not trained are
among the growing numbers in classes for behaviour
problems, special schools, the juvenile court, or mental
hospitals. Because they are unable to cope with accepting
responsibility in the real world, they try to escape with
dope, alcohol, sex, or rebellion.

Surprisingly, many of these undisciplined and unhappy
young people have been taught what is right. However,
when those who have taught them do not require them to
face reality and act responsibly, young people conclude
that what they have been taught is not really important. Or
they come to feel that those who have taught them do not
care enough to make them do right.

Real love demands discipline. God sets the pattern in His
own dealings with us. His Word teaches:

> For whom the Lord loveth, he chasteneth and scourgeth every
> son whom he receiveth. If ye endure chastening, God dealeth
> with you as with sons. . .but if ye be without chastisement,
> whereof all are partakers, then are ye bastards and not sons
> (Hebrews 12:6-8).

If we love our children, we must teach them what is right.
We must also train them to do what is right by consistently
applying penalties whenever they do wrong. Teaching with

training will not permanently alienate children. God's Word says:

> Now no chastening for the present seemeth to be joyous, but grievous: nevertheless afterward it yieldeth the peaceable fruit of righteousness unto them which are exercised thereby (Hebrews 12:11).

To teach a child takes time. To train him so that he does not end up an insecure, mixed up, learning-disabled child or a self-willed, rebellious teen-ager takes a whole lot more time, love, and patience.

IT TAKES TIME FOR PLAY

Most "teaching" of preschool children is not done in any sort of structured, scheduled, classroom way. Much of what a preschooler learns intellectually and achieves physically is mastered while playing. A small child does a great deal of this play while alone. However, some of it needs to be done with the intelligent, guided direction of a loving parent.

It takes time to provide a child with freedom to explore and play creatively in a home. Giving enough supervision to keep a child safe and out of trouble while he explores takes time and vigilance. Yet this time must be invested. There is a great deal about life and his world that a fourteen-month old cannot learn while confined to a playpen. Constant "hovering" is neither necessary nor good. However, it does take time to "babyproof" areas of the home, maintain enough supervision, and provide stimulating skill-building playthings. These are not necessarily toys. In "babyproofing" the home, everything movable cannot be removed. A baby needs access to "things." For example, your child will learn important lessons such as relationships of size by having access to four or five pans and skillets of assorted sizes or other unbreakable containers which will "nest." Important physical skills will develop as the child "plays" with these items. Clothespins and a bottle will capture a child's interest and build skills in another way.

Playing simple games with children as they develop and grow takes time but it is important. Children are given varying levels of intelligence (ability to perceive and reason) by God. Others He gives the physical "equipment" to excel in music, sports, and similar areas.

Everyone is given enough basic ability for the place God
has for them in the world. The "winners" in life are not
those with the greatest ability. Success goes to those who
have developed what God has given them and use it to the
fullest potential. A lot of that development---physical,
mental, and emotional---takes place in play during the very
early years. To give the child the opportunity for the right
kind of play, to supervise that play, and to get involved
occasionally takes time.

A FULL-TIME JOB

Being a parent is a full-time responsibility---24 hours a
day---365 days a year. In the Bible God shows us this when
He says:

> And these words which I command thee this day, shall be in
> thine heart: And thou shalt teach them diligently unto thy
> children, and shalt talk of them when thou sittest in thine
> house, and when thou walkest by the way, and when thou liest
> down, and when thou risest up (Deuteronomy 6:6-7).

Training a child involves saturating both our own life
and his in the character building principles of the Word of
God---and requiring him to do them. This is a day-in, day-
out lifetime commitment. It is not even complete when our
own children are raised for God says:

> ...teach them thy sons, *and thy sons' sons* (Deuteronomy 4:9b).

That all takes time---years of time.

THE MISSING INGREDIENT

Raising children does take time. However, the reduced
amount of time parents spend training children today---
or even their lack of know-how is not the biggest single
factor which produces character deficiencies and learning
disablement.

The real problem is that for twenty years or more so many
parents have cared so little. Had they cared more, they
would have taken the time and gotten the know-how to
shape and influence their children's lives in the right
direction. In fact, the care which comes from true love will
also make up for any deficiencies in time and know-how.
The Bible teaches this. It says:

> And above all things have fervent charity [love] among

yourselves: for charity [love] shall cover a multitude of sins. (I Peter 4:8).

This Scriptural promise is a real comfort to parents who know that they cannot be perfect. True love keeps them trying. It will also "cover a multitude of sins (short-comings)." Unfortunately, however, this kind of true love is hard to find in today's society.

True love is not a feeling. True love is giving---the giving of one's self to meet the needs of others. True love was described by the Lord Jesus when He said:

> Greater love hath no man than this, that a man lay down his life for his friends (John 15:13).

That is the kind of love He had for us. It is the kind of love which causes a person to put aside his own wants and desires to help and serve and please the one he loves. It is this kind of self-sacrificing love that husbands and wives need for each other and their children. With this kind of love parents give the time needed to meet all of the physical, emotional and spiritual needs of their children.

All people, young and old, need love and the assurance of it continually. When that love is missing, tragedies result. As the years pass without true love, children become part of . . .

> . . .the millions of unloved, hurt, sullen, rebellious children who try to escape with rock music, drugs, and sex. As the pressures grow they take out their frustrations by assaulting 70,000 teachers a year and destroy $600-million in school property through senseless vandalism. One million of the most desperate run away from home each year and 15,000 kill themselves---part of the 400% increase in juvenile suicides in 20 years.

The "missing ingredient" is love. The kind of love and giving of self which would prevent such tragedies and heal the hurts and wounds they have already caused takes time.

IT IS TIME TO DECIDE

Raising children takes time. It requires the time of both father and mother. Will you dedicate yourself to taking the time to do it right? Will you dedicate yourself to take the time to read---the time to teach---the time to train---the time to play---and the time to love? Your decision will determine your child's future success and happiness. And also that of your grandchildren.

Chapter III

1. Copyright 1969, Zondervan Publishing House, Grand Rapids, MI.

GET A VISION

Where there is no vision, the people perish...therefore my people are gone into captivity, because they have no knowledge.

--Proverbs 29:18, Isaiah 5:13

HAVE YOU EVER really stopped to think that presidents George Washington, Thomas Jefferson and Abraham Lincoln were once little babies like yours? So was Thomas Edison, the inventor of the electric light bulb. The Wright Brothers, who flew the first airplane, and the great black scientist, George Washington Carver, also started life as babies.

The English preacher John Wesley probably had a greater long-range impact on English and American history than did any other man of the last 250 years. Wesley began life as a baby. So did Adolf Hitler, Karl Marx, Judas Iscariot, the Revolutionary War traitor Benedict Arnold and President Kennedy's killer Lee Harvey Oswald.

For every Washington and Wesley, there are millions of other babies whose names are not in history books. But they grew up to be happy, successful, productive people in their own quiet way. For every Hitler, Marx or Oswald there are millions of others who have grown up to struggle through lives of frustration and failure, turmoil and tragedy.

What these babies grew up to become---good or bad---was largely shaped and determined by the training and love and encouragement they received---or missed--from the time they were infants. So will it be with your child. The Bible says:

Train up a child in the way he should go: and when he is old, he will not depart from it (Proverbs 22:6).

Those who have been the greatest help to the world, or
their country, or their families have usually come from
homes where parents had a real vision for their children.
George Washington's parents, for example, gave themselves to training their son. They did not set out to train him
to be president of the United States. They did train him to
have the basic character qualities which would make him
happy and successful wherever he would find himself in
life.

William H. Wilbur, in his excellent little book, *The
Making of George Washington*,[1] points out that Washington
was neither the smartest nor the most talented man of his
time. Rather, he says. . .

> . . . The difference between Washington and his contemporaries
> was a fundamental one; it was a matter of greater moral
> character and real worth. These are qualities which, although
> built and developed throughout life, can only be attained in
> maximum degree if initiated at a very early age.

Washington's parents had a vision of what kind of
person they wanted their son to be. They then dedicated
themselves to training him. His father, for example,
traveled to England when George was four and spent time
learning how to plan and supervise George's education.

Biographers report that Washington's mother "gave
herself unstintingly to her children." She was particularly
dedicated to teaching George to obey. However, as General
Wilbur shows in his book, it was Washington's father,
Augustine, who really trained and shaped his son's
character and life. The father drilled the character-building
lessons into his son that he had received himself in
England's Appleby School. Young George started memorizing Scripture including the Ten Commandments, at a very
early age. From his father young George learned such life-
shaping maxims as:

> It is not sufficient just to obey---you must learn to obey
> cheerfully. . .obey first: and ask questions later. . .Accept
> corrections thankfully. . .Labour to keep alive in your breast
> that spark of celestial fire called conscience.

The "copybooks"---the notebooks---in which young
George did his lessons are displayed in the Library of
Congress. In one, completed when he was about twelve,

George Washington wrote again and again the "Rules of Civility and Decent Behaviour." Some of the more than 110 which were recorded in his own carefully practiced handwriting were:

> Do not repeat news if you know not the truth thereof. . .Speak not evil of the absent. . .Let your conversation be without malice or envy. . .Speak not injurious words either in jest or in earnest. Scoff at none though they give occasion. . .Associate yourself with persons of good character. . .It is better to be alone than in bad company. . .

> In disputes, give liberty to each one to present his opinion. . .Be attentive when others speak. . .Be not obstinate in supporting your own opinions. . .Think before you speak.

> When a man does the best he can, yet succeeds not, do not blame him. . .Show not yourself glad at another's misfortune. . . If anyone comes to speak to you while you are sitting, stand up, even though you may consider him to be your inferior. . .If you meet a person who is your elder, yield to him the path or right of way. . .In writing or speaking always give to every person his due title.

These rules build courtesy, wisdom, and kindness. They give ample evidence that Augustine and Mary did not intend that George should wander through life picking up standards and habits, good or bad, wherever he might encounter them. His parents took steps to be sure that George first learned the right way, the honest way, the courteous way, the moral way. George was required to learn the rules. He believed in them and tried his best to obey them *all of his life.* An eminent Washington scholar, Charles Moore, has written:

> These maxims were so fully exemplified in George Washington's life that biographers have regarded them as a formative influence in the development of his character.[2]

The author of *The Making of George Washington* adds: "The lasting effect on Washington was largely a consequence of the fact that *the rules were sponsored and enforced by his parents.*" General Wilbur told how they did it:

> . . .the philosophy of training and character development which was used on George with such signal success, was based on an intelligent combination of (1) the assembly of a large

number of reasonable, easily understood, sensible do's and
dont's (2) the calm and uniform insistence on compliance with
all of them, and (3) certain correction or mild punishment every
time that George failed to comply. He thus acquired both very
sound habits and highly developed sense of responsibility.

Washington's father died when young George was just
eleven years old. The boy missed the father tremendously---
but the father had done his job well. Father Augustine's
legacy to his son, as William Wilbur said so well, was. . .

> . . .a philosophy, a set of standards and convictions that guided
> Washington throughout his life. . .Truly the legacy which
> George received from his father was a heritage of moral
> character, integrity and wisdom.

The "Father of Our Country," as far as we know, never
attended school. He got his basic education from his
parents. He progressed rapidly and was studying geometry
and trigonometry by the time he was twelve. (His father
believed that the study of mathematics helped develop a
logical, reasoning mind.) He was a successful surveyor by
the time he was 15, commander-in-chief of the Virginia
militia at twenty-one. He got his college and university-
level training on his own under the supervision of an older
brother in about five years. The brother had Washington
read the lives and philosophies of great men and the history
of Persia, Rome and Greece. He was the commander-in-
chief of the American army in the War for Independence,
chairman of the Constitutional Convention, and the first
president of the United States. A quick survey of one
biography reveals the following as some of the words used
to describe his character. . .

> . . .obedient, responsible, contented, faithful, honest, neat,
> moral, truthful, a logical reasoning mind, attentive, teachable,
> gentle, self-controlled, frank, straight-forward, modest,
> humble, inquisitive, well balanced, patient, worked without
> supervision, self-reliant, determined, reverent, and respectful.

Truly George Washington's entire life is a testimony that
the Proverb is correct which says:

> Train up a child in the way he should go: and when he is old, he
> will not depart from it.

Washington's parents had a vision of what they wanted

their son to be---and they worked to bring it to pass.

THE PREACHER WHO CHANGED HISTORY

John Wesley was twenty-nine years old when Washington was born. He died at eighty-seven---two years after George Washington became president. If his own mother had not trained him to do the will of God whatever the cost, George Washington might not have had the opportunity to write his name so brightly into the pages of our history. Washington's great character and ability might never have been recognized except for Wesley. History might have taken a completely different direction--- except for John Wesley.

Wesley was a preacher. He preached all over England. He rode horseback from town to town to preach over 100,000 messages during his eighty-seven years. He made the long, hazardous journey across the Atlantic a dozen times. He was so dedicated to fulfilling his responsibilities that he was known to walk six miles to a preaching engagement when he was eighty-five years old.

God raised him up at a time when England was on a verge of social, economic, moral, and military collapse. Through the Bible preaching of a handful of men led by John Wesley, England was turned away from the revolution which was to destroy France a generation later. His preaching produced revival and reformation in the cold, dead existing churches of the day. A new world-wide Gospel-preaching church which took the name of "Methodist" resulted from his work. Even though less than 2½% of the population of England was converted through Wesley's sixty-year ministry, the face of England was changed. That handful became the "salt of the earth." They turned back corruption and purged the land of moral decay. The whole course of English and American history was changed.

In 1922, British Prime Minister David Lloyd George stated that Great Britain. . .

. . .owed more to the movement of which Wesley was the inspirer and leader, than to any other movement in the whole of its history. . .It civilized the people. . .There was a complete revolution effected in the whole country. . .it has given a different outlook to the British and American people from the outlook of the Continentals.[4]

Lord Baldwin, during his term as prime minister in the late 1920's, said that historians. . .

> . . .who filled their pages with Napoleon and had nothing to say about John Wesley now realize that they cannot explain nineteenth century England until they can explain Wesley. And I believe it is equally true to say that you cannot explain 20th Century America unless you understand Wesley.[5]

As the words of the two British prime ministers indicated, the Wesley revival spread to America in the 1740's. It produced the moral climate in which young George Washington grew up. The Wesley revival also created the spiritual foundation in individual Americans which made them willing to follow George Washington's principled leadership. That's why the thirtieth President of the United States, Calvin Coolidge, said:

> America was born in a revival of religion. Back of that revival were John Wesley, George Whitefield, and Francis Asbury.[6]

Wesley was totally dedicated to doing God's will in God's way during his eighty-seven years of life. His life is a testimony to what a dedicated mother with a vision for training her children can accomplish.

Susanna Wesley had nineteen children. John was the fifteenth. Susanna was an amazing woman. She fed and clothed her children. She ran the family farm and taught Bible classes as a pastor's wife. In addition to all of these full-time jobs, she served as her children's elementary school teacher. She also disciplined herself to give each one of her children one hour a week of her undivided attention and time. Her disciplined life paid off. John's preaching and dedication sparked the revival that changed the face of England and America in the 1700's---and the direction of world history for 250 years. Another son taught for twenty years in one of England's finest universities. We still sing the hymns of her youngest son, Charles Wesley.

The year George Washington was born, John Wesley was twenty-nine years old. Wesley asked his mother that year to set forth in detail the method of education she had used to train him and his brothers and sisters. After repeated requests, she agreed. As a result, we have a detailed record of the wisdom and dedication of this 18th Century mother. In a letter on July 24, 1732 she wrote:

> According to your desire I have collected the principal rules I observed in educating my family.
>
> The children were always put into *a regular method of* living in such things as they were capable of, from their birth; as in dressing and undressing, changing their linen. . .a regular course of sleeping, which at first was three hours in the morning, and three in the afternoon; and afterwards two hours till they needed none at all. . .Drinking or eating between meals was never allowed, unless in case of sickness which almost never happened. . .They were so used to eating and drinking what was given to them that when any of them was ill there was no difficulty in making them take the most unpleasant medicine.

It was a structured, disciplined existence. Biographer William Fitchett in his book, *Wesley and His Century*, commented that John Wesley's childhood was set up "on the principle of a railroad timetable." The training paid off. As a man Wesley was always conscious of the value and importance of every minute. To give her children this orderly, disciplined life, Susanna Wesley had to discipline herself carefully. Her biographer, Rebecca Lamar Harmon said:

> The wonder is that any one person could have maintained such a schedule as Susanna Wesley set for herself.[7]

CONTROLLING THE WILL

The key to Susanna Wesley's entire child training program was bringing the child to accept authority as early as possible. In the same lengthy letter she wrote:

> I insist on conquering the child's will because when this is thoroughly done, then a child can be governed by the reason and piety of his parents, till its own understanding comes to maturity, and the principles of religion have taken root in its mind. I cannot yet dismiss the subject. As self-will is the root of all sin and misery, whatever cherishes this in children ensures their after wretchedness and irreligion: whatever checks it and mortifies it promotes their future happiness and piety.

Mrs. Wesley told why she deemed it so very important when she wrote:

> The parent who indulges the child's self-will does the Devil's work; makes religion impracticable, salvation unattainable, and does all that in him lies to damn his child's body and soul forever.

The practice which Mrs. Wesley termed "conquering the will" might at first glance appear to mean breaking the spirit of the children. This was not so. As her biographer wrote:

> Like the training the military gives, Susanna's stringent regime was not simply for more efficient handling of a large group of people, but as better preparation of each member of the company for the battle of life ahead. Her system was always geared to the future when each individual child should have reached a state of maturity and could regulate his own life. The formation of character was ever the goal of all her striving.

Susanna Wesley was wise enough to know that her children could never recognize her love, benefit from her wisdom, and enjoy her fellowship until they had accepted her authority. Susanna's entire program for the training and development of her children was motivated and wrapped in love. Mrs. Harmon records:

> Nowhere is there any record of resentment on the part of the Wesley children against their mother's method of education. In fact, John tried to carry out her plan to the letter in his Kingswood School. [8]

DEVOTIONAL LIFE

As soon as the Wesley children could speak they were taught the Lord's prayer which they said upon arising and at bedtime. As they grew older, a short prayer for parents was added. Doctrinal teachings and Bible verses were committed to memory. They were taught very early to recognize that the Lord's Day is different from other days and that they were to be still during family prayers. Psalms were sung at the beginning and end of school. The older children were trained to help the younger ones come to a reverence for God's Word.

A LIFE LONG COMMITMENT

The education of the Wesley children was not finished when they left home. Both the father and mother followed them wherever they were with letters of wise counsel. The children held the parents in deep affection. Love dominated the relationships of the family circle. When he was eighty-one years old and had long been the most famous preacher in the world, John Wesley wrote of his deep yearning to see Epworth, his old family home, again. "Epworth," he wrote," which I still love beyond most places in the world."

How did Susanna Wesley achieve this life-long love and affection in her children? How did she accomplish the "formation of character which was ever the end of her striving?" In initially resisting son John's request to record her plan of education for others to use, she gave the secret. She said:

> The writing anything about my way of education I am much averse to. . .No one can, without renouncing the world, in the most literal sense, observe my method; and there are few, if any, that would entirely devote above twenty years of the prime of life in hopes to save the souls of their children, which they think may be saved without so much ado, for that was my principal intention, however unskillfully and unsuccessfully managed.

Susanna Wesley dedicated herself totally and completely to making her children fit for Heaven and the service of God. In the process she gave them the character they needed to succeed in this life as well. Her sacrifices, which look so large, were richly rewarded in her own life---and in the blessings her children have been to the world ever since.

Susanna Wesley knew what she wanted for her children. She dedicated herself to forming the character within them so that they could achieve the goals she set.

What do *you* want for *your* children? Do you know? Have you gotten a vision of what they could be---what they could become? Do you have a goal? Or will your child just "grow up?"

Do you want your baby to be polite and mannerly and obedient? Do you want your child to be reverent and respectful? Do you want your son or daughter to love you and trust you and enjoy your fellowship?

Do you want your child to have character? Do you know what character is? Someone defined character as that quality of "doing right even when you don't feel like it." Do you want a child who is responsible and has a desire to achieve? Do you want your son or daughter to grow up interested in the world and what is happening? Do you want a truthful child—a contented child?

None of these things will just "happen." Children are born disorganized and self-willed. They can become what ever you are willing to dedicate yourself to making them. Your baby can be a blessing to you—and the world. He can be blessed himself in the process but you must be willing to give yourself totally to developing his character. Susanna Wesley is an example of the "persistence" which is required. Her husband, Samuel Wesley, listened as she worked to teach a bit of information to one of the young children. As she repeated the lesson again and again, he impatiently interrupted to say: "I wonder at your patience. You have told that child the same thing twenty times." She replied:

> If I had satisfied myself by mentioning it only 19 times, I should have lost all my labour. It was the twentieth time when the lesson was finally learned.

Will you give yourself to developing the same dedication and determination?

Chapter IV

1. *The Making of George Washington*, Copyright 1970 and 1973, William H. Wilbur, published and distributed by Patriotic Education Inc P.O. Box 1088, DeLand, FL 32720
2. Ibid., pg. 111
3. Ibid.
4. Quoted by Bready, *This Freedom Whence?* Pg. 96-97
5. Ibid., pg 97
6. Ibid., pg xv
7. R. L. Harmon, *Susanna, Mother of the Wesleys*, Copyright, Abingdon Press, Nashville, TN
8. Ibid.

Chapter V

START RIGHT NOW!

See then that ye walk circumspectly, not as fools, but as wise, redeeming [using] the time, because the days are evil. Wherefore be ye not unwise, but understanding what the will of the Lord is.

---Ephesians 5:15-17

DO YOU NEED some encouragement to dedicate yourself to making the same effort made by the parents of Washington and Wesley? Do you need a further challenge on the importance of starting *right now*? The Bible records the amazing stories of two families who had to give up their sons when they were only four or five years old. From then on they grew up under very unwholesome influences. Even so, both little boys became giants for God and blessings to their nation. *Before they were five they received the essential basic training they needed to succeed in life.* They did not depart from it when they were older. Let's look briefly at the stories of Moses and Samuel.

THE TRAINING OF MOSES

When Moses was born, his people, the Jews, were in slavery in Egypt. Pharaoh, the Egyptian ruler, had just decreed that all Israelite boy babies should be thrown into the river and drowned. He feared that if the Israelites continued to multiply, they might get too strong for their captors.

Moses's parents hid him for three months after he was born. Then they put him into the river in a little ark. Pharaoh's daughter found the infant. "By chance" she hired Moses's own mother to nurse him. Moses stayed with his mother until he was weaned (at about age four or at most five in those days). From then on he was reared in Pharaoh's household and was trained to be the ruler of

Egypt someday. He grew up with all of the luxury and opportunity for sin available in the palace of a wicked, heathen king. However, his early training paid off. The New Testament tells us:

> By faith Moses, when he was come to years, refused to be called the son of Pharaoh's daughter; choosing rather to suffer affliction with the people of God, than to enjoy the pleasures of sin for a season; esteeming the reproach of Christ greater riches than the treasures in Egypt, for he had respect unto the recompence of the reward. By faith he forsook Egypt, not fearing the wrath of the king: for he endured, as seeing him who is invisible (Hebrews 11:24-27).

Really examine that passage. See all that it reveals. As a result of the few early years of training that Moses had before he was five years old, when he grew up, he. . .

> . . .knew who the people of God really were—knew that while sin offers pleasure it only lasts "for a season"—knew and believed about the coming Messiah (Christ)—correctly evaluated that heavenly rewards are of greater value than earthly treasures— knew that the invisible God could protect him from the anger of an all-powerful earthly king—and had the character to do what was right no matter what it cost him.

This is an amazing record. It is a fantastic testimony to the value of early childhood training. The Bible says that all of these things which Moses knew and did were "by faith." The Scriptures teach that "faith cometh by hearing . . .the Word of God." Moses's only opportunity to have heard and been taught the Word of God was during the few years he was at his mother's breast. There is not even a possibility that he found an old Bible in the corner of Pharaoh's library as he was growing up—for the Bible had not yet been written.

A careful study of the record shows clearly that Moses's early training kept him from being contaminated by the worldly teaching in Egypt as he grew up. The training he received from his parents before he was five years old also determined how he would live and the important choices he would make for the rest of his life. The story of Moses is a dramatic illustration that the Scripture is true which says:

> Train up a child in the way he should go: and when he is old he will not depart from it (Proverbs 22:6).

Moses's mother and father believed God and made good use of the short time which He gave them to train their son.

THE TRAINING OF SAMUEL

Little Samuel was an answer to prayer. After years of being unable to have children, Hannah asked God for a son. She promised to train any boy God would give her to serve the Lord all of his life. God answered her prayers and gave her a son. The Bible records that she. . .

> . . .gave her son suck until she weaned him. And when she had weaned him [certainly by the time he was five] she took him up with her, with three bullocks and one ephah of flour, and a bottle of wine [for the sacrifice] and brought him unto the house of the Lord in Shiloh: and the child was young. And they slew a bullock, and brought the child to Eli [the priest] (I Samuel 1:23-25).

The mother left the little boy with the aged priest. The Scripture says that she went back "from year to year" to worship and to bring him new clothes as he grew.

Eli's home, where little Samuel lived, was not an ideal place for a child to be reared. Eli's sons are described in the Bible as "sons of Belial (the devil)." They "knew not the Lord." They stole the best meat from the sacrifices people brought to offer God and ate it themselves. They caused public scandal as they "lay with the women that assembled at the door of the tabernacle of the congregation." Eli did not discipline his sons—even after God sent a special messenger to rebuke him and tell him that thou "honorest thy sons before me." This was the aged man into whose hands the boy Samuel was placed when he was just four or five years old. However, even under this unwholesome influence the scripture records that. . .

> . . .the child Samuel grew on, and was in favour both with the Lord, and also with men. . .and the Lord was with him, and [Samuel] did let none of his words fall to the ground (I Samuel 2:26, 3:19).

Little Samuel carefully kept all of God's Word and went on to be a mighty man of character and a prophet of the Lord. About the only sound training he could have received was what his mother gave him in the years before he was four or five years old (until he was weaned). He did not

depart from it when he was old. Samuel's life is a testimony
to the truth of the Bible promise which says. . .

> Train up a child in the way he should go: and when he is old he
> will not depart from it (Proverbs 22:6).

Parent--will you see the tremendous opportunity and
responsibility you have to shape and form your baby's life?
You have just a few short years before the time for school
comes! Will you dedicate yourself right now to becoming an
instrument in God's hands for training your child for His
glory and service?

If you want to do right, God will teach you what to do. He
will show you what you and your home need to be to train
up your child in the way of the Lord.

Perhaps you are going to have a baby sometime in the
next nine months. Or maybe you have just brought your
little one home from the hospital. In any event it is not too
early to start getting ready for school and life.

What you do and don't do in the first few months and
years of your baby's life will have a life-long impact. You
will be shaping your child's personality, character,
emotional behavior, and ability and desire to read. Actually
you can even start getting your child ready for school and
life even before he or she is born. Both the Bible and the
"experts" indicate that your attitudes and actions even
during the months before the birth have a real impact on a
child's life.

We probably have no idea how much a baby in the womb
may know and feel and store up in his developing little
mind. Experts have determined that babies hear and react
at least three months before birth. By monitoring responses
of infants before birth, Swedish scientist, Dr. E. Wedenberg,
determined that. . .

> . . .in the 24th week of intrauterine life, the fetus is listening all
> the time.

A New Zealand expert on prenatal physiology, Dr. Albert
Liley, has found that the baby hears "outside" noises as
early as the 28th week of pregnancy. These experts are just
"discovering" what the Bible said 2000 years ago! The
Bible records that three months before John the Baptist
was born he recognized the presence of the Lord Jesus

Christ in the womb of the Virgin Mary. The scriptures say that after Mary learned from the angel Gabriel that she was to conceive a child of the Holy Ghost that she. . .

> . . .arose in those days, and went into the hill country with haste, into a city of Juda; And entered into the house of Zacharias, and saluted Elisabeth. And it came to pass, that, when Elisabeth heard the salutation of Mary, the babe leaped in her womb; and Elisabeth was filled with the Holy Ghost.
>
> And she spake out with a loud voice, and said, Blessed art thou among women, and blessed is the fruit of thy womb, And whence is this to me, that the mother of my Lord should come to me? For, lo, as soon as the voice of thy salutation sounded in mine ears, the babe leaped in my womb for joy (Luke 1:39-44).

The findings of the experts and Bible teachings show the importance of starting early to surround your child with right influences. Maintain the right attitudes toward them. Get excited about cultivating the potential in their lives. This book was written to (1) show the vital importance of starting your child right. (2) the tragedies which can result from waiting too long and (3) to give encouragement and guidelines for being a knowledgeable, wise, loving parent.

If your baby is already past one of the "crucial" milestones, do not despair. Learn as quickly as you can. Make corrections in the way you train and relate to your child as soon as possible. Then trust our gracious God to repair any damage done through past ignorance or omissions.

TRAINING THE WHOLE CHILD

> *I pray God your whole spirit and soul and body be preserved blameless unto the coming of the Lord Jesus Christ.*
>
> *--I Thessalonians 5:23*

RECOGNIZING that a child has three "parts" to his total being is the starting place for effective child training. Man is composed of body, soul, and spirit. In the process of a child's growing up, each of his three "parts" must be stimulated, fed, trained and exercised.

Each of man's three "parts" is triune also. Man's *body* is made up of flesh, bones and blood. Man's *soul* consists of his mind (where he stores information, thinks, and reasons), his emotions (where he feels), and his will (where he decides). Man's *spirit* also has three "parts" with differing functions. It is through man's spirit that he "knows" himself. Through his spirit he knows or senses the things of man. The spirit is also that part of man into which God's Spirit comes to live at the time of salvation. Having God's Spirit dwelling in his spirit enables a person to know and understand the things of God.

Man has this triune makeup because he was made in the image of God. God is a trinity. He is one God who exists eternally as three persons---Father, Son, and Holy Spirit. Man, having been created in God's image, is also triune--- with the three "parts" making up the whole person.

Each "part" of a person affects the function and operation of the other parts and the whole. For example, doctors and scientists have discovered that a chemical imbalance in a person's body will affect his thinking, his emotions, and his behavior. The reverse is true also: What a person thinks in his mind will affect his emotions, how he feels physically, how he acts, etc. The emotions, if not properly controlled, can upset the body and cause chemical imbalance, physical exhaustion, sugar problems, high blood pressure, ulcers, etc.

Problems in the spiritual part of man will cause serious physical problems also according to the Bible. When Israel came out of slavery in Egypt, for example, God told them:

> If thou wilt diligently hearken unto the voice of the Lord thy God, and wilt do that which is right in his sight, and wilt give ear to his commandments, and keep all his statutes, I will put none of these diseases upon thee which I have brought upon the Egyptians: for I am the Lord that healeth thee (Exodus 15:26).

Disobeying God is one of about seven reasons the Bible gives for poor health.*

In both the Old and New Testaments, the Bible shows that spiritual problems affect man's health, emotions, etc. Clearly all the "parts" of man---his body, soul, and spirit---are interrelated. All must be developed properly for balanced growth.

All three "parts" of a baby's being---the body, soul, and spirit---have needs for food, stimulation, training, and exercise all through life. Some "parts" have greater needs at some times than others. Yet the "parts" cannot be divorced from one another and dealt with separately any more than the three persons of the Trinity can be separated. The Father, Son and Holy Spirit are three persons---yet they

----

*To stay healthy, it is important to recognize why people get sick. Doctors deal only with symptoms. If the real cause of an illness is overlooked, the symptoms will often recur or show up in another area of life. The seven Bible reasons for sickness include: (1) disobeying God's natural laws (not enough sleep, poor hygiene, overwork, wrong food, poisoning our bodies with tobacco, alcohol, etc.) In Philippians 2:25-30, a man named Epaphroditus "was sick nigh unto death . . . for the work of the Lord." Overwork, even for a good purpose, can cause sickness. (2) Disobeying God's spiritual laws will also cause sickness. God promises that He will not put the same sickness on His people who obey Him as He puts on the world. See Exodus 15:26 and 23:25. (3) In I Corinthians 11:27-30, some people were sick and others were already asleep (dead) because they merely went through the motions in partaking of the Lord's Supper. (4) Children can get sick and even die because of the sin of

are one. To know or approach any one of the three is impossible without recognizing them all. The Lord Jesus, for example, said:

> No man cometh to the Father but by me. . .he that hath seen me hath seen the Father. . .I and the Father are one (John 14:6,9 and John 10:30).

Jesus and the Father are two persons, yet they are one. We cannot understand this. But because the Bible says it, we accept and believe it. The Bible also reveals that the Holy Spirit and Father are one. In the Bible account of the birth of Jesus Christ, an angel appeared to Joseph and told him:

> Joseph thou son of David, fear not to take unto thee Mary thy wife: *for that which is conceived in her is of the Holy Ghost.* And she shall bring forth a son, and thou shalt call his name JESUS for he shall save his people from their sins (Matthew 1:20-21).

Jesus was conceived by the Holy Spirit. So actually, the Holy Spirit is the Father. Again we see that while the Father, Son, and Holy Ghost are three distinct persons—they are one God. We cannot understand it, but we must believe it because the Bible teaches it.

It is impossible to divide the Trinity. So, too, it is impossible to dissect man and deal with his "parts" separately. For example, the Bible speaks of man's conscience. Every man knows he has a conscience even though he may ignore it until it is almost totally inoperative. And while all men have a conscience, it is impossible to locate it definitely as being in one or another of man's

---

their parents. See II Samuel 12:13-23. (5) Hatred, particularly of God's people can bring sickness. See Deuteronomy 7:15. (6) Satanic attack can cause sickness and physical afflictions. See Job 2:1-8, Luke 13:10-17, Acts 10:34-38, and II Corinthians 12:1-10. (7) The deterioration of our bodies, sickness and aging are the result of the accumulated effects of sin in the human race. It is used ultimately to end physical life and take the lost to judgment and the saved to heaven.

Not all sickness is the result of sin. For example, in John 9:1-3, a man was born blind, not because of his own sin or that of his parents, but so that God could show His power in healing him. In John 11:4 the Lord said that Lazarus's sickness and death were for the "glory of God." It was permitted so God could show His power in raising Lazarus from the dead. It is important to realize that all sickness has a purpose in God's eternal plan for our lives.

"parts". The conscience is part of man's total being. It is not just a function of the brain or the mind, although both are involved. It is not just a function of a person's emotions, although the emotions are involved. It is not just a function of the spirit, although the spirit is involved. The conscience reflects the fact that man is made up of many parts---yet he is one complete being.

Proper development of body, soul, and spirit will require attention to be focused on the needs of each "part"---while always being mindful that each "part" affects the other parts which make up the total person.

THE BODY

From being almost totally helpless at birth, a baby must develop a fantastic number and range of physical abilities and skills in a few short years. From being nearly immobile, a child must learn to wave his arms and kick his legs, randomly at first and then with some coordination. He will develop the ability to turn over, sit up, crawl, walk, and then run. He must start focusing his eyes on an object, grasp objects which he sees, and finally learn to coordinate the various parts of his body so that he can manipulate spoons, forks and knives in eating and pencils and crayons in scribbling and then drawing and writing.

He must learn to use and control his tongue, his lips, the throat muscles, and his breathing to produce noise and sounds and then control the sounds to reproduce words which he hears with his ears. Control of bodily elimination functions and dressing himself are among the host of other physical skills to be learned and mastered.

Almost all children develop these basic abilities. How coordinated and skillful children will be in carrying them out will depend on the encouragement and opportunity they get.

THE SOUL

Because a new baby's physical needs are so pressing and so obvious parents may neglect the development of the soul and spirit. Then one day they will find that they do not have a sweet-tempered little member of the family. Instead, they will have either a little "monster" who rules the house with selfish, whining and a domineering spirit or a broken, shy,

fearful, retiring child. To avoid these tragedies, parents
need to start forming an obedient will within the child from
the time of birth. Children must be challenged and trained
to analyze, reason, think, and make sound decisions. They
need to learn that choices have consequences.

They must learn how to recognize and respond to love
and react to hurts. They need to be developed into warm,
outgoing little people who will grow up to love and be loved.

THE SPIRIT

From birth and before a child's concepts of himself,
others and God are being formed in his spirit. Lifelong
attitudes of self-acceptance or rejection, feelings of security
or insecurity, and loving faith or bitter cynicism toward
God and others start forming.

SUMMING IT UP

Almost all children are born with enough physical,
mental, emotional, and spiritual capabilities to excel in
some way. Whether they ever achieve their potential
depends on whether the whole child gets the right start.
Without it, a child with all of the basic capabilities can end
up an uncoordinated oaf physically, be a mental sluggard,
be fearful of making decisions or will make them rashly
and have a "don't care" or skeptical attitude toward man
and God.

Having the proper long-term developmental goals for the
whole child can avoid these tragedies. Day-to-day activities
can then be carried out to give your baby the needed
experience to develop desired abilities, skills and character.

Much of what a baby needs to develop and learn in all
three parts of his being will come "naturally" as parents
provide normal, common sense, day-to-day care. However,
parents need to be mindful of what "normal" care really is.
They need to realize how limited a child is at birth (in
ability and experience). They also must have some idea of
what the baby needs to become as the months and years
pass. Most of all, parents need insights into how a child's
environment stimulates development.

A Missouri school superintendent wrote to parents in his
school district in an effort to show that having challenging
experiences from infancy on makes a difference. He said:

Take two babies with equal gifts and intelligence. Leave one to lie in his crib for hundreds of hours staring at a blank ceiling while the other has interesting-to-look-at things tacked to the ceiling or hanging from his crib and spends waking hours being jostled, cuddled, talked to, sung to and played with. *Which child is starting life with an advantage?*[1]

After asking this almost self-answering question, he continues:

As they leave the crib to crawl and then to toddle, expose one to accidental learning while the other is encouraged to explore, experiment and engage in skill developing and thought-provoking games. *Which child enters school the best equipped to succeed?* And equally important, which child is most apt to live his daily preschool days feeling happier about himself meeting each new day's experiences with greater self-assurance?[2]

If children do not have the opportunity to experience the things which they need to develop skills at appropriate ages, they will always have a degree of handicap. Overly cautious mothers, for example, may not give children the opportunity to use muscles and develop coordination from infancy on. Their children may always be somewhat clumsy no matter how they may work to make up the skills later. An expert on the physical and psychological development of a child explains why:

If appropriate stimuli are lacking in early infancy then the potential for developing certain skills, abilities, and characteristics gradually disappears.[3]

That concept was explained in layman's language in the introduction to *Games to Grow On,* a series of helps for parents of pre-school children prepared by the Ferguson-Florissant school district in Missouri. According to the booklet, a child is born with a built-in time table which. . .

. . .makes him especially "ripe" for learning or developing certain things at certain times. If a child does not acquire a particular skill when he or she is "ripe"- - -a greater effort is required to master it at a later age. For example if a child is not adequately exposed to language during the peak language period from 18 months to three years---it will take longer and be harder for him to make up the difference later. *In fact, sometimes the gap is never closed.*[4]

The same truth applies in the early years of school. Most children are ready to learn to read when they start kindergarten. If they are not taught to do so, they will never really develop full potential no matter how much remedial effort is put forth later. This is a Bible concept. The Word of God teaches:

> To every thing there is a season, and a time to every purpose under the heaven (Ecclesiastes 3:1).

The importance of developing skills in sequence can be better understood by looking at several illustrations. In the physical area, for example:

> Without large muscle development a child will never run, pick up a pencil, or throw a ball. Every parent should recognize this. Not as many are aware that without on-time "tuning" of small muscles the child may walk but will appear to be an un-coordinated oaf who falls over his feet. He can pick up the pencil but will scrawl when he writes. He can toss a ball but won't throw one strike out of ten.

Similar step-by-step, on-time development in the use of the senses is important also. For example:

> To learn to read and speak most effectively, a child needs to see and hear. Just as essential, however, is the development of *discerning* seeing and hearing which distinguishes small differences in shape, size, appearance, and sound. Without this "fine tuning" of vision and hearing, the child will be handi-capped in distinguishing between a "b" and a "d", a "p" and a "q" or an "m" and a "w" on the printed page or the slightly different sounds of a "b" and "p" and other sound-alikes.

While recognizing the importance of doing the right thing, the right way, *at the right time*, parents should not panic and become fearful. The "exercises" and "learning experiences" that a child needs are chiefly just those which he or she will get in the course of living and growing up with parents who love him, care for him, spend time with him, play with him, challenge him, and enjoy him.

The following pages will give a brief survey of some of the normal things and fun things parents can do to help a child achieve the potential God has for him. These guides should serve to stimulate creative parents to devise appropriate and interesting activities for children from birth to age five.

THE HELPLESS TIME: 0-3 MONTHS

At birth, and for a number of weeks thereafter a baby seems totally helpless. The obvious needs are physical. For several months a baby mostly just eats and sleeps. The instructions of your own doctor are normally the best guide to follow in meeting these needs.

A baby gets needed "exercise" during the first several helpless months while being routinely changed, bathed, fed, burped, etc. It takes place naturally *if* the parent is not too timid, too busy, or too business-like to play for a few minutes four or five times a day.

New parents who tend to be overly cautious sometimes find a safe, secure way to hold the new infant and stick with it. However, babies are not very breakable. They can and should be given some variety in the way they are handled. Remember though that the head and neck do need support during this period.

As soon as possible the child should have freedom while in bed to kick his legs, and wave his arms without the restraint of tight clothes or tucked-in blankets. Such lively, spontaneous movements stimulate circulation, breathing, digestion, and other bodily functions. Building of muscles and the coordination of their movements start also as the child is free to move.

Vary the Environment: The baby's bassinet can be turned "head-to-foot" daily (or the baby positioned differently in the crib) so that the light source and sounds come from different directions at different times. This exposes the baby to the idea that he lives in a varying, changing environment. At some point during the day when the baby is awake (less than 20% of the time at first) carry the bassinet with you from room to room as you work (or use an easy-to-move car seat).

Along with these changes of environment and attention, plan to let the baby have some awake periods to himself. Everyone needs to learn to be alone. Babies should not become accustomed to being "entertained" or with others during every waking hour. Children can easily become very demanding of attention.

Stimulate the Senses: Babies need things to see and opportunities to practice focusing the eyes. Drape brightly colored things---a tie, a ribbon, or other "eye-catchers"---on the sides of the crib. Start when the child is about two weeks old. Change the object and its location about once a week. In the same way, introduce occasional noise-makers---a rattle, a toy which squeaks, or place a ticking clock by the bed for an hour or so each day.

By about six weeks most children will react if a brightly colored object is moved through their line of vision. First they will obviously focus on it. Later they "follow" it as it moves.

Most such physical stimulation and challenging of the senses is just the result of doing what comes naturally---but it is important.

Awakening the Soul: During this early "helpless" physical time, the needs of the baby's soul (mind, emotions, will) cannot be neglected. The emotions need to be nurtured with love. Babies need to be held, cuddled, talked to, kissed, caressed, and told, "I love you!"

The thought processes and the will need stimulating. Talk to the baby while he is being fed. Give instructions such as "all right now, open your mouth," as the baby's lips are brought into contact with the nipple. As the baby takes the nipple and begins to nurse, the child can be told, "That's right---that's a good baby." Actually, the baby is born with a built-in reflex so that the mouth opens and sucking starts as soon as anything touches the lips. As the baby grows, however, the reflex is replaced by learned behavior. Through the process of talking, instructing, and encouraging, the first steps are taken toward building the decision making and obeying "process" into the will.

This sort of verbal instruction, encouragement, and approval should continue as the baby develops. The early start is a training process for both the child *and* the parent.

Starting to play good music as soon as you come home from the hospital may help your baby to grow faster, be healthier, and better adjusted. A study by the University of California Medical Center in Los Angeles found that premature babies who have Brahms, Beethoven, etc. played for them grow faster and get out of the hospital earlier and healthier. Five hospitals across America participated in the study. The new-born babies thrived when the classics were played four times a day for ten minutes each time. However, exposure to rock music caused them to be agitated and compounded the stress they experienced from entering the world prematurely.[7] In view of the studies cited in Chapter V on how babies hear in the womb from the 24th week of pregnancy, expectant mothers should also be careful about the music their yet-to-be-born children hear.

Most of these "instructions" may seem overly elemental. However, we are living in a time when some babies lie in their cribs day by day without stimulation. They are handled unemotionally (or with irritation). They are rarely talked to. For example, it is impossible to measure the long-range emotional damage done when a mother impersonally feeds a baby while watching TV rather than talking to him.

Spiritual Development: The development of the spirit should begin during these same "helpless" months. The spirit is that part of the total being where a person "senses" things about the world and others and where he knows himself. The spirit is also that part of man into which God's Spirit comes to live at the time of salvation. Through his spirit man knows God and the things of God.

The development of a healthy spirit begins as a baby "senses" that all is well. He gets this "sense" from a mother who is calm and at peace with herself and the world around her. The baby "feels" a sense of security in his spirit when parents are in agreement and at peace with one another. That these relationships in a baby's environment are "right" is vitally important.*

Short passages of Scripture should be read to the baby after he or she has been fed, burped, changed, and is ready to go back to sleep. The parent should pray with the child. A child gets his first idea of the existence of a God who cannot be seen when the mother or father kneels by the crib and prays for wisdom and strength in caring for the baby. At

----

*Detailed help for obtaining personal peace and maintaining unity in the home is given in Chapters 10-14.

some point the baby will sense something special in voices lifted up in prayer. Gradually the baby will learn that parents are talking to a Person who is present but not seen. As the baby grows he will come to understand the words of praise and Thanksgiving. He will see the trust of his parents. He will grow in the knowledge that God has great power and is worthy to be praised and loved. He will learn that God can be trusted to protect and provide. The short "devotional" time can end with singing of a quiet hymn like "Jesus Loves Me" or "What A Friend We Have in Jesus."

Reading Scripture and praying and singing hymns to an infant may seem ridiculous—but it is God's way. There is a sound Biblical precedent for starting very early. We have already seen the examples of Moses and Samuel. There are others. In II Timothy 3:14-15, the Apostle Paul, told Timothy to set himself apart from the wicked age in which he lived by continuing. . .

> . . .in the things which thou has learned and hast been assured of, knowing of whom thou hast learned them: *And that from a child thou hast known the Holy Scriptures*, which are able to make thee wise unto salvation through faith which is in Christ Jesus.

The New Testament was written originally in Greek, the "official" language of the entire Mediterranean area 2000 years ago. The Greek word translated "child" in this passage is *brephos*. It appears in the Scriptures only five other times. In two cases, the word is translated "babe" and it refers to John the Baptist *while he was in his mother's womb* (Luke 1:41 and Luke 1:44). In two other cases, also translated "babe," the word refers to Jesus Christ when He was a newborn infant in swaddling clothes lying in the manger (Luke 2:12 and Luke 2:16). In the fifth case, the word refers to "infants" who were so young that the disciples objected to having them brought to the Lord Jesus by their parents. Evaluating all these passages shows that Paul was saying that Timothy had "known the scriptures" (with his senses) since he was an infant. He had been exposed to the Word of God by his mother. It was stored up in his mind and working in his spirit while he was just a babe in arms.

Infants should have the Bible read and quoted to them. It cannot hurt them. And we cannot know how early the Word of God will start having its effect on the new little person.

Dr. Jack Hyles, pastor of the giant First Baptist Church of Hammond, Indiana, tells that as soon as his children were brought home from the hospital he would sit by their beds and tell them that the book he was holding was God's Word. Then he would start reading from Genesis 1...

> ...in the beginning God created the heaven and the earth.

He says, "It sure couldn't hurt them and I wasn't taking any chances on waiting too long." In his book, *How to Rear Infants*,[5] he recalls that his own mother used the same procedure in training him. He writes:

> I do not recall when she started it; I do know she started this practice long before I could comprehend what was going on, but as far back as I can remember I can see my mother teaching me that Jesus is God's Son and that the Bible is God's Word.

Starting a regular devotional time early in a child's life is an important priority. It starts the building of lifetime habits. The intellectual development of the child is stimulated as well.

The importance of such early training is confirmed by the child development specialist, Dr. Jaroslav Koch. In his book, *Total Baby Development*, Dr. Koch says:

> ...an unsuspected and exciting potential for development lies hidden and untapped within infants... many opportunities for development are lost because mothers and fathers don't give them a chance to unfold.

> Insufficient knowledge of the psychological development of infants has been the main cause for the notion that it is impossible to communicate with a newborn and that upbringing can begin only after he acquires some ability to reason...Research has shown that an infant should be trained from his very first days of life and that he becomes more responsive the better he is reared during early infancy---and, of course, later too.[6]

The most alert three-month-old child I have ever observed was a baby whose mother started reading the Scriptures (and other things) to him within days after his birth. So--- start training your baby---and have fun while you do it!

BECOMING A PERSON: 3-8 MONTHS

This age is, in a way, the most delightful time in a baby's

life for the parents. Much of the anxiety that new parents experience has passed. They have found that the baby does not break very easily, and can therefore be played with. If colic has been a problem, the baby has just about grown out of it. He is not mobile yet and does not have to be watched constantly. He is just fun. The weeks unfold and. . .

> . . .baby starts to lift her own head just a bit. Then your little girl starts to support herself upright and looks around as she is held. When talked to, she'll break into a smile. She obviously responds to people. She's so interested and yet so quizzical as you talk to her.
>
> Your boy lies in the crib and looks at his toes and waves his arms and occasionally swats or kicks a ball suspended overhead. At first the contact is accidental but he develops his aim as the months pass.
>
> Soon baby will be babbling sounds. If you repeat the sounds the child makes, by about six or seven months you can be having "conversations." While you should repeat the sounds a baby makes when you talk, do not use "baby talk" or that is the way the child will learn.

During the early middle part of this period, baby will start to grasp things which are offered---fingers, plastic rings, rubber toys, etc. As the period progresses, give the child additional objects of various sizes, shapes, and colors. With "practice" the baby will focus on objects and follow them as they are moved through space. Calling the child or "squeaking" toys from different directions gives practice in turning in the direction from which sounds come.

Given the opportunity the baby will exercise himself but you should help. When changing diapers grasp the feet and do a bicycling routine. As the child is able to grasp the fingers on one of your hands, pull him up a few inches as he hangs on. As the baby progresses, carry out this routine and then grasp his feet with your other hand. Lift the child a few inches off the table, being sure there is a soft padding underneath the head area when his finger grasp slips. Once he can sit up by himself he can spend a few minutes at a time in a jumping seat. This develops leg muscles.

As the eighth month approaches, the child will be able to sit up with support, "stand" when held, look at himself in the mirror, may play peek-a-boo, hold a cup with a handle, roll from back to stomach and vice versa, and imitate some of your actions. Obviously, the "helpless time" is over.

At about seven or eight months, when the baby's attention is attracted to an object, or person, name it. Later as a child associates several different objects with their names, games can develop. Early steps toward obedience training can start by teaching the meaning of "yes" and "no." After the child associates several objects with their names, practice naming the object. When the child looks to it, say, "Yes" with obvious approval. If the child looks at the wrong object, say, "no...no...no" with mild disapproval. Develop other "games" to start teaching and re-inforcing the meaning of "yes" and "no."

During this period the child should also be developing the ability to relate to other people. If you have been attending church regularly, your baby will be handled in the nursery by several people other than his parents. Developing relationships outside the family in this way can be a pleasant rather than a disturbing experience.

Continue to surround the baby with love. Make the Lord and His Word a vital part of the daily routine. Do not neglect a devotion time with regular Bible reading and prayer. Have "thanksgiving" before meals and for other appropriate happenings. Continue to have some good music playing in the home each day. It will help baby and you. Use traditional classics (Bach, Beethoven, Handel, Haydn) and the good old hymns.

Good music helps develop a quiet, peaceable spirit in a person. The Bible says so. About 1000 years before Christ, Israel's first king (Saul) rebelled against God and was afflicted by an evil spirit. His servants had a remedy. The Bible says:

> And Saul's servants said unto him, Behold now an evil spirit from God troubleth thee. Let our lord now command thy servants, which are before thee, to seek out a man, who is a cunning player on an harp: and it shall come to pass, when the evil spirit from God is upon thee, that he shall play with his hand, and thou shalt be well (I Samuel 16:15-16).

A young shepherd boy who knew the Lord and His power was recruited to play. The Scripture tells us:

> And it came to pass, when the evil spirit from God was upon Saul, that David took an harp, and played with his hand: so

> Saul was refreshed, and was well, and the evil spirit departed
> from him (I Samuel 16:23).

Good music does heal a troubled spirit. The reverse is also
true. After Moses was given the Ten Commandments by
God he came down off the mountain. The children of Israel,
meanwhile, had made an idol. They had formed a golden
calf and were worshiping it in defiance of God's law. As
Moses and Joshua neared the camp, the scripture tells us:

> And when Joshua heard the noise of the people as they
> shouted, he said unto Moses, There is a noise of war in the
> camp. And he said, It is not the voice of them that shout for
> mastery, neither is it the voice of them that cry for being
> overcome, *but the noise of them that sing do I hear*. And it came
> to pass, as soon as he came nigh unto the camp, that he saw the
> calf and the dancing. . .and Moses saw that the people were
> naked (Exodus 32:17-19a, 25a).

The music and singing which accompanies idol worship
and lewd partying sounded like "noise." Missionaries
report that modern "rock" music has the same beat and
sound as the "music" primitive people use in their worship
of evil spirits.

To develop a peaceful, reverent spirit in your child (and
yourself), fill your home with music—but make sure it is the
right kind. Be careful about the sound and the beat, even if
the music has religious words.

READY TO GO: 8-15 MONTHS

This new period will, in many ways, be the most important
learning time in baby's life. It will also be the most
challenging for parents (particularly the mother). During
these next eight months your son or daughter will. . .

> . . .begin to crawl, then walk and even climb. The newly
> developed mobility will be used to explore *everything*. No
> longer will baby be totally dependent on you. He or she will find
> you and anyone and anything else he wants. At times you will
> be driven almost frantic. Along with mobility also comes the
> ability to open drawers, jars, bottles and boxes, eat from a
> spoon, drink from a cup, etc.

To develop fully the new ability to move around, your
baby needs freedom. Freedom is also needed to satisfy the
curiosity which is so important to learning. While the child

needs freedom, he has not yet learned to assume the responsibilities or understand the restrictions which must go with it. There is seemingly no comprehension of danger. This all poses a real challenge to parents. Fortunately, at this age, along with mobility your child will also. . .

> . . .give evidence that understanding of the meaning of some words is developing along with the ability to reason—to think and make rational decisions. He will also start to say some words. As the months pass he will understand and respond to a lot more words than he can say. These evidences that intellectual abilities are appearing give hope that the child can be taught some limits on what is safe and unsafe and what is acceptable conduct and what is not.

As baby comes into this challenging new age, safety of the child is the parents' first responsibility. At the same time, children must be given freedom to develop their new mobility fully and satisfy the curiosities which develop. Activities must be planned which will further stimulate the child's physical, intellectual, emotional and spiritual capacitites. Wow! What responsibilities—but that is not all!

At the same time, the authority of the parents must be established. This is a delicate operation which can only be performed with the determination, persistence, insight and the care which real love gives. *The child's will must be brought under control while using care not to break the child's spirit.* The child must be encouraged to be curious, to know, to explore, to find out about the world around him. He must also start to learn that all curiosity cannot be satisfied. This will protect him in later life when he wonders what sort of experience marijuana or other drugs give—or why *Playboy* has such an attraction for other boys. It will protect the young teen-age girl when she begins to wonder how it would feel to be touched by a boy. Curiosity is so important to learning. It can also bring disaster if uncontrolled.

The total weight of all these needs and responsibilities can bring a parent to cry, "It's impossible!" However, if God gives you children, He has called you to train them. He promises. . .

> . . .faithful is he that calleth you, who also will do it (I Thessalonians 5:24).

Tragically many parents give up. They do not know how to look to God to direct in the child raising process. By eighteen or twenty-four months parents find themselves with a little monster on their hands. It is that stage which parents and baby books call "The Terrible Two's."

Almost every baby book says it is inevitable. It is unless children are brought to accept authority and discipline at about the time they learn to walk. Otherwise, they become impossible as they near the second birthday. Dr. Burton White's preschool research project at Harvard, for example, discontinues home visits and observations of children during the half year or so when open rebellion is worst. Most of the books assure parents that children will "get over it" or "grow out of it."

What actually happens is that parents develop compromises that are workable for a time. However, these will eventually break down when the child must submit to authority somewhere. This case history illustrates what happens:

> According to observations made from the time Jimmy was about two, he was a well-mannered, well-behaved, very "grown up" little boy. His parents had apparently done a super job. He was very interested in the world. He had an advanced vocabulary and looked like a super prospect for kindergarten. We were very surprised, therefore, in the early weeks of school when the teacher reported encountering real stubbornness, lack of cooperation, and rebellion in the classroom. The "mystery" was solved when it was realized that the mother had always treated her son as "a little person." Any time the mother wanted the child to do anything she patiently explained how it would be to the child's advantage to cooperate and "obey." If a problem arose in public, the mother would quietly take the child aside for a consultation and the difficulty would be resolved. The child was usually well-mannered, compliant, pleasant to be around, etc. because he was usually smart enough to see that it was to his advantage to do the right thing. He did the right thing not because he was obedient and had actually accepted the authority. He obeyed because he saw it was to his benefit to do so. He was actually in charge---he was the final authority.
>
> The absence of an obedient heart became obvious when the little boy encountered an old-fashioned kindergarten teacher who was the authority in the classroom and expected obedience

because she was in charge. The child's stubborn will which had never been brought to submission rebelled. A number of difficult months followed until the child came to accept authority because it was authority.

There is a very fine line here—but it is an important one. It is good, when possible, to see that children understand reasons for your requests. Understanding brings a whole-hearted obedience. This is illustrated in the Bible. The psalmist prayed and asked God:

> Give me understanding, and I shall keep thy law; yea, I shall observe it *with my whole heart* (Psalm 119:34).

However, children must be trained first to obey immediately and without question *whether they understand or not*. Their lives may, in time, depend on such obedience. Long before children learn anything about electrical theory, they must obey instructions not to put fingers or other objects into electrical outlets. Children should learn that respectful questions can be answered *after* they cheerfully obey.

Most modern child-training experts do not understand the importance of bringing a child to accept authority. Instead, they advise parents to avoid confrontations by "bribing" children into compliance. For example, if a young child has picked up something which is breakable or could be dangerous, the "experts" almost unanimously advise offering him something in trade. This may avoid a confrontation; however, training children to obey cannot be done without some "confrontations." In an emergency a "trade" may be a life saver but do not let this practice become a habit.

Most outright rebellion and obstinate stubbornness will not manifest itself until after the 8-15 month age period. If it is to be prevented from developing, however, the job must be done during this crucial time.

When are children "ready" to be trained to obey? The groundwork is laid from the time they are born. Children start learning from the beginning when you are pleased and when you are not. A parent continually shows approval or disapproval by the tone of voice or facial expression. As you show love you are building the basis for discipline. Starting "Yes-No" drills at about eight months gives a firmer foundation.

At some point, usually between nine to twelve months of age, you will know that your child has a rather good idea of what you want. However, you will also see and sense that a conscious decision has been made by the child to "do his own thing." He is not a confirmed, hardened rebel at this point. He is just testing you. This is the occasion for the first spanking. This is not cruelty or child abuse. Firm action, at the right time, avoids the need for much painful hassling later. This is why John Wesley's mother, when describing how she raised her children, said:

> When turned a year old (and some before) they were taught to fear the rod. . .by which means they escaped abundance of correction which they might otherwise have had later.

Once the child's will was brought under control the job of developing an understanding in the mind could proceed in an orderly fashion. Mrs. Wesley said:

> In order to form the minds of children, the first thing to be done is to conquer the will and bring them to an obedient temper. To inform the understanding is a work of time, and must with children proceed by slow degrees, as they are able to bear it; but the subjecting of the will is a thing which must be done at once, and the sooner the better, for by neglecting timely correction they will contract a stubbornness and obstinacy which are hardly ever after conquered, and never without using such severity as would be painful to me and the child.

By modern standards, Mrs. Wesley's program may seem very harsh. She explains why her method (the Bible way) is the kindest in the long run. She wrote:

> In the esteem of the world they pass for kind and indulgent whom I call cruel parents, who permit their children to get habits which they know must afterwards be broken. . .When a child is corrected it must be conquered and this will be no hard matter to do, if it be not grown headstrong by too much indulgence.

Not taking firm, persistent action early will later produce the stage called, "The Terrible Two's." Children should be spanked for any deliberate, willful, knowing disobedience--- for disrespect, backtalk, insolence, etc.---and for lying. Older children should also be spanked for foolishness.

Mrs. Wesley achieved obedience without nagging children

about every little detail all the time. She advised:

> When the will of a child is totally subdued, and it is brought to
> revere and stand in awe of the parents, then a great many
> childish follies and accidents may be passed by. Some should
> be overlooked and taken no notice of, and others mildly
> reproved; but no wilful transgression ought to ever be forgiven
> children without chastisement less or more, as the nature and
> circumstances of the case may require.

The discipline process should usually be started "full
force" when the child becomes mobile. This is a necessity. It
is also the right time. God has planned the maturing
process so that the child is capable of responding to
discipline at about the same time he becomes mobile.

Most baby books recommend giving a child maximum
freedom to roam and to explore. This is wise. Keeping
children confined to a playpen or crib for hours on end is
stifling. However, before giving the baby the freedom to
"roam," experts advise that the home be "child-proofed."
What they generally mean is that anything and everything
breakable or dangerous be removed. This lets the child be
free of any restrictions. This is a questionable practice from
the standpoint of the child's overall development. Naturally,
no parent with any sense is going to turn a child loose in a
house with bottles of poison, open razor blades or bare
electric wires readily available to the toddler. Neither will
the wise parent leave priceless family heirlooms within
easy reach--- any more than he would start a child practicing
the use of a cup for the first time with a fragile china cup.

However, children should be trained from the start what
they can touch, use, and explore and what is off limits. Dr.
Jack Hyles in his excellent book, *How to Rear Infants*,
describes how he started training his four children. He
says:

> When our children first learned to walk, I took them on a tour of
> the house. I pointed to certain objects and said, "No, no, no, no,
> no, no!" I did this until the children associated the objects with
> "No!"

When a child crossed over into forbidden territory, Pastor
Hyles says:

> I then proceeded to let him know that pain was associated with
> disobedience. I did not take a stick and hit the child; neither did

> I beat him with my fist, but lovingly and gently and tearfully I
> used the place God provided for spankings, and I gave him a
> spanking with whatever intensity I felt the crime demanded.
> The intensity should not be determined by the anger of the
> parents or the discomfort that the crime caused. It should be
> commensurate with the crime.

The wise parent should not start out making too many
demands. A very small child's capacity to remember is
limited. However, parents must be extremely diligent in
requiring the child to fulfill *all* demands which are made. In
the process, the child learns that whatever the parents say
is law. This is the key to broadened obedience later. Every
child will test—often a number of times—to see if the parent
really means what he says. Consistency in discipline will
quickly bring a child to a place of cheerful obedience and a
place where understanding and cooperation can be achieved
through words or even just a "look." Constant paddling is
not required. With some children a few early firm spankings
establish patterns of obedience which last a lifetime.
Others are more stubborn.

As a child grows and develops there will be times of
further "testing" (even into the teen years). At these testing
times, the authority of the parents will have to be reinforced.
If, however, the lessons are properly taught early and are
consistently and lovingly reinforced through the years, a
baby can grow into a happy, obedient, loving person.

WHY SPANK?

Spanking has come to be regarded as "child abuse" in
some areas of the United States. Therefore, parents should
know how to spank to avoid excesses which would rightly
be dealt with by law. It is also important to know how, why
and when to spank in order to achieve the desired Scriptural
results.

First of all, spanking is not just permitted by the Bible—it
is required. The Word of God says:

> He that spareth his rod hateth his son: but he that loveth him
> chasteneth him betimes (Proverbs 13:24). Withhold not cor-
> rection from the child: for if thou beatest him with the rod, he
> shall not die (Proverbs 23:13).

Spanking has a number of definite long-range benefits

for the child. Proverbs 20:30 says that it cleanses away evil and aids in the development of a clean inner life. Other benefits are deliverance from foolishness, the obtaining of wisdom and a happy future life. The Bible says:

> Foolishness is bound in the heart of a child; but the rod of correction shall drive it far from him. (Proverbs 22:15). The rod and reproof give wisdom: but a child left to himself bringeth his mother to shame (Proverbs 29:15).

There are other important benefits for the here and now and for eternity also. Proverbs 23:13-14 says:

> Withhold not correction from the child: for if thou beatest him with the rod, he shall not die. Thou shalt beat him with the rod and shall deliver his soul from hell.

A child who learns to obey may be spared from death someday. If you teach your eleven-month old to obey instructions about the dangers of electrical outlets now, he will listen to and follow other safety instructions exactly on the job when he is grown. An obedient child who learns not to go into the street now will grow up to follow speed laws, etc. Each of these qualities may help save his life now or in the future. A child who has learned that all disobedience on earth is punished will understand God's message that sin demands a penalty. Such a child is prepared to trust that Christ has already, paid the sin penalty on the cross and wants to be the child's Saviour.

HOW TO SPANK

Spanking is commanded by God. It should not be carried out in anger or with an attitude of getting even with a child. Therefore, when a child commits an offense for which spanking is a penalty, the wise parent should make a brief prayer the first step in the disciplinary action. By taking the time to pray, the parent gives God an opportunity to correct any wrong attitudes. He also opens himself to the leadership and guidance of God's Spirit if there should be some unusual circumstance in the situation requiring attention. Discipline should never be an automatic routine.

After prayer, the child's guilt should be established. A very small child should be faced with his offense. Older children should be required to state *what* they have done (not why).

Before applying discipline, parents should establish their authority. "Johnny, do you know that God says I have to spank you because _____?" Quote an appropriate verse from Proverbs to establish the need for the spanking. Establish that you must apply discipline because of your love for him. You can tell the child, "I love you too much to let you go on doing wrong. I must spank you because it will help you to do right in the future."

The child should then be spanked *on the bottom only*. *Never* slap a child's face or strike other parts of the body, pull hair, or drag by an arm. The paddling should be administered privately. For small children some advise using the hand. Others recommend something like a ping pong paddle. The Scripture says that a "rod" is to be used. This could be interpreted to be something like a switch. Some parents have found that purchasing a ⅛" or 3/16" dowel from a hardware store or lumber yard permits applying the "rod" in a Scriptural way. A rod stings sharply and will apply "stripes" to the flesh. Before rejecting the use of a "rod" or switch which cannot do permanent physical damage, realize that a parent's hand can be a lethal weapon.

Use the rod hard enough and long enough to make the child cry---and until he gets over any anger which is shown when the rod is applied. (Mrs. Wesley required her children to "cry softly"). The paddling should be long enough and hard enough to outweigh the pleasures of sin.

When the spanking is completed, give the child a few minutes to calm himself. Then discuss the offense with him. (The Scripture says "The rod *and* reproof give wisdom ...") Then move to re-establish fellowship. The child should be brought to ask for forgiveness and it should be granted. One wise father required his sons to thank him for administering the spankings they needed. Assure the child of your forgiveness (which means you will not bring up the offense again) and your love.

After prayer and any final brief words of encouragement, get things quickly back to normal. Dual penalties such as a spanking plus banishment of a child to his room are counter-productive.

Be reasonable in what you expect from your child. The

Scripture commands and warns:

> And ye fathers, provoke not your children to wrath: but bring
> them up in the nurture and admonition of the Lord (Ephesians
> 6:4).

If the Scriptural pattern for disciplining children is
followed carefully and consistently, the rod will not have to
be used often. Applied correctly it is effective. Once your
authority is established, then be careful that children
always know what you expect. They should also know the
penalties for breaking any rules. If you find yourself
having to spank again and again for similar offenses, ask
God to show you why the discipline is not producing
promised Scriptural results.

DEVELOPING OBEDIENCE

Spanking, of course, is not the only tool or "pressure"
used in establishing authority and training children to be
obedient. If used with the right loving attitude and at the
right time, it will make the other aspects of obedience
training a blessing---and a lot easier, too. "Pressures" other
than the physical kind include (1) the pressure of the
responsibilities you give to children, (2) the pressure exerted
by the *expectations* they know you have for them, (3) the
pressure to measure up to the *example* you set for them by
your life, (4) the pressure to measure up to the example of
the right heroes, (5) the pressure of *consistency* as they
always know what to expect from you, and (6) the pressures
created by *praises, rewards and penalties*.

Each of these "pressures" is important. However, the two
strongest pressures or incentives for your child to obey will
be (7) the knowledge of your *love*---and (8) and *awareness
of God's presence*.

When loved, a child (usually) wants to please the one who
loves him. A growing consciousness and awareness that
God is living in and through you will also build a desire in
the child to "do right."

FUN AND GAMES

During these months children love to knock down a tower
of blocks and then build them up again. (Ability to knock
down comes before the ability to build up.) They are
enthralled by emptying and filling containers, things

which nest inside each other, and a drawer which is "theirs" to empty and refill. A cabinet section with a hinged door (so that it swings) gives fun and learning at the same time. These activities help to develop coordination and finger dexterity.

A "game" which builds the habit of obeying has the children on command do such things as. . .

> . . .clapping the hands, waving bye-bye, pointing to a ball or other named objects, passing a toy back and forth on command, etc.

These all help to train the child to respond to your commands. Each is normally developed one at a time. After each one is mastered individually, a drill can be conducted using a series of varied commands one after another. Variations can be introduced. For example, when passing a toy or other objects back and forth on command, saying "Please" and "Thank you" on each exchange can be added to the exercise.

Play "Where's the _____?" with actual objects and people in the room and in picture books. (Always be careful at first to use the same terms in describing things and people.) As the child becomes more mobile, put him to "work." Practice having the child bring you a nearby small item. Naturally this activity follows ability to crawl, grasp, and hold items. The game can be varied as the child grows by "hiding" the item under a blanket while the child watches so that to bring the item he must remove the blanket first. Another later variation would be to have an assortment of three things for the child to choose from when commanded to bring one of the items.

The baby does not need your attention and stimulation all of the time. Spending five to eight minutes several times a day on similar but varied activities will do wonders in stimulating the development of physical, intellectual, social, and spiritual abilities and interest. Most important, give the baby the opportunity to experience a varying environment of shapes, textures, and colors. Interests in things and their varying characteristics fascinate children at this age.

DEVELOPING SPIRITUALLY

Since birth, your child has been exposed to Bible reading,

prayer, and spiritual songs. As you near the end of this period, the baby can start to cooperate in spiritual exercises. The baby can be encouraged to bow his head, close his eyes and fold his hands at prayer time. If the child is not ready to follow these instructions, do not make a big thing out of it. If a child is not ready to keep his eyes closed do not let open eyes interfere with your own sincere attempts to communicate your feelings and desires to the Lord. Remember too, a child's attention span at this age (even when you can get his attention) is very, very short. It is not the time for reading pages of Scripture or praying with him for all the world's needs!

GOING STRONG: 15-24 MONTHS

The months ahead will be a joy and blessing, or a trying time. It will all depend on the foundation you have laid. During the days ahead, your child will. . .

...begin to run (wobbly at first)---go up and then down stairs (if you have any)---seat himself in a small chair---throw a ball--- turn the pages of a book (in bunches at first)---obey simple commands---develop the ability to use about 20 words (and understand several hundred)---carry out two step directions--- find and point to pictures in a book (and later name the item pictured).

Your child will be able to take off some of his or her clothing (socks, hat, shoes)---sometimes to your dismay! As the period proceeds, the child can and should be taught to pick up toys and put them away. Your son or daughter will use a cup (with both hands) and a spoon. The child will begin to show signs of possessiveness over certain items, particularly if there are slightly older brothers or sisters. Your child will play alone contentedly if you are around. A sand box and opportunity for water play are favorites. The outdoors expands the child's world. Even as his world expands, the child also tends to cling to mother and is torn between the need to explore and the need for security. Because children at this age are real mimics, be careful what you do and say.

Exploration is the theme at fifteen months just as growing interest in mastering of skills or using a toy will be for the two year old. Rather than playing with a toy or object, the child in this period will be occupied thoroughly by looking at all sides of an object, banging it, dropping it, spinning it, biting it, or turning it. A child's play may seem aimless---but it actually makes a big contribution to physical development and mental growth.

Day-by-day growth and development in every area will amaze and thrill you. At the same time, life will become "impossible," particularly if during the previous period your authority was not established and the child's will brought under control. Even if you did an adequate job then, there will be much testing during this period. Strive, therefore, for consistency in every area. Maintain your authority and expand the areas in which you can expect your child to obey. Restudying pages 64-73 is a good idea at this point.

Toilet Training: This is another subject over which the "experts" differ widely. Almost everyone says, "Don't rush it." They differ greatly, however, on what "rushing it" means. Some experts say not to start toilet training until the baby is 18-24 months old to avoid making demands which the child is not physically or emotionally able to cope with. At the other extreme, Dr. Jaroslav Koch in *Total Baby Development*[7] recommends a program which supposedly can achieve toilet training by the middle of baby's second year. Apparently the more early opportunities a baby is given to develop physical skills and an awareness of what is happening in and around him, the sooner he will be toilet trained. There are three key developments on the road to toilet training. The child. . .

> . . .will first develop the ability to tell you when an elimination has been completed. Next, he will be aware and able to announce to you that he is in the process of eliminating. (This can be frustrating because it is still too late to help.) The third stage is when the child recognizes the feelings which precede elimination and can announce it in time.

At each stage, the child should be praised and encouraged for telling you. Do not ever scold the child for dirtying himself. However, if you find him wet or dirty *without telling you*, let him know your displeasure that he didn't tell you.

The cycle can be speeded up by recognizing times when elimination usually takes place and putting the child on the pot. Whenever successful timing is "arranged" show the child what has been done and give lots of praise. However, do not keep your son or daughter sitting for long periods.

Start the proceess by encouraging the child to let you know as soon as diapers are dirtied. As soon as the baby learns this step encourage an announcement when elimination is taking place. Work toward the third stage—the time when there is a recognition of impending elimination.

Exerting undue pressure will cause the child to get anxious about toilet training and the ordeal will be prolonged. Generally, the longer you wait to start toilet training, the quicker the job will be accomplished. Do not rush into the project because you are "sick and tired of diapers" or want to keep up with the timetable of friend's children.

Language Development: During this period and the next one your baby will begin to comprehend and use much of the basic vocabulary and grammar which will be used during all of life (except for technical words). Your child is now using "name" words. As the baby approaches age two, encourage the combining of "name" words with "action" words to make short sentences. The most effective way to develop language skills is to talk, talk, talk. Identifying what your child is really interested in at the moment is actually the key to stimulating conversation. Be careful to pronounce words distinctly, speak in complete sentences, use good grammar, and avoid slang. Doing so will have a big influence on how precisely your child speaks all through life. Start working at two-way conversations as this time proceeds.

Do not rely on the TV to teach your child language. He will do a lot better with opportunities for two-way communication with you. Dr. Burton White says:

> Exposure to TV programs like *Sesame Street* probably will, in a modest way, have an impact on the child's level of language development, but rest assured if he never sees a single television program he can still learn language through you in an absolutely magnificent manner.[7]

Any benefit which might be learned from TV is far outweighed by the exposure to disrespect, violent actions and foul language. Such conduct is a particular problem on the cartoon shows. Your child will be happier and more content and read earlier and better if he never starts watching TV.

Continue reading to your child. Do not just read stories. Stop and talk about the pictures and what is happening. Get your child involved in conversations about story happenings.

Another fun way to develop language skills comes from making a pair of mitten "puppets" from socks. Paint or sew "faces" on them. Make one for your hand and one for the child. Back-and-forth conversations between the two characters help develop imaginations (for child and parent) and language ability. Talk about the activities of the day and about likes and dislikes. *Do not ever glorify "bad" characters or tolerate disrespect even in these "play" situations.*

Physical Development: Supply your child with containers having lids, blocks, cans, balls, and other items in a variety of shapes to stack and sort. Sorting objects by shapes into piles will help the child develop skills which will eventually enable him to discriminate between letter shapes on the printed page.

Crayons for scribbling on large pieces of paper are also encouraged at this age and will enable the child to start developing finger dexterity. A few empty cartons make "neat" houses, tunnels to crawl through, etc. In fact, the best "toys" are probably those a creative mother devises from available "junk."

Another fun-type developmental activity starts with simple puzzles made by cutting magazine pictures into three irregularly shaped pieces. Then show the child how the pieces fit together. As the child grows in age and ability, puzzles can be made progressively a little more complex (cut one piece into two parts).

Thinking Ability: Along with physical development, children need to start developing thinking ability. To some extent, this comes "naturally." Children will also make more progress, however, if they "exercise" their developing capabilities. Provide opportunities and challenges for problem solving. Ferguson-Florissant school district in suburban St. Louis pioneered in the development of some excellent help for parents to use in stimulating the thinking process during the preschool years. Their three-year Parent-Child Early Education Program includes a whole series of "Games to Grow On." These "games" are common sense ideas which give the child the opportunity to start solving problems and overcoming obstacles. These are the first steps in the thinking process. Several which might help the creative parent to develop his own "Games to Grow On" are:

> HIDE 'N SEEK: Any hide 'n seek game presents a problem to be solved. Let the child watch as you cover a toy under one of two or three differently colored towels. Or, the object can be hidden in one of two or three boxes or bags.
>
> STRING PULL: Attach strings to two towels or handkerchiefs. Place a toy on one towel and hand the child the strings and say, "Get the toy."
>
> A STICK IS A TOOL: Seat the child at the table and place a toy out of reach on the table. Make a small stick available within arm's length and ask the child to get the toy. Demonstrate, if necessary how to use the stick.

These games are problem-solving mind-stretchers that also provide practice in hand-eye coordination. Learning does not happen instantly. Children master skills by practicing them over and over just as they will someday learn to add numbers, form letters, or recognize basic sounds. Allow them to make mistakes without making a big thing of it. Praise effort (however feeble it might be) whenever children are learning new skills. Give recognition for the slightest progress and the smallest accomplishment. One of your earliest goals should be building your child's self-confidence. Always remember, too, that children develop at different rates.

Spiritual Development: Daily devotional times, prayer before meals and at bedtime and hymn singing should continue. For many months now, the child should have been mimicking you in folding hands to pray and bowing the head when expressing thanks.

There is, of course, no substitute for the parents' example in developing reverence for God in your children. If the Lord is real to you, you will talk about Him in all of your

daily activities. As you do, God will become as real to your
child as other family members are.

PUTTING IT TOGETHER: 24-36 MONTHS

As this new period begins, you realize that your "baby"
has become a "person." A lot of the "budding" skills,
abilities, and interests for which you have been looking
will blossom out during this year. By the time your "baby"
reaches three years old, he or she will exhibit a degree of
mental maturity and exercise a level of control over his
emotions and body which would surprise you right now.

By the third birthday, a child will walk, run and climb
with confidence not shown at age two. He will ride a tricycle
fairly capably if he has been given an opportunity to
develop the skill. He will enjoy using the backyard swing
and slide. At the start of the year your child will negotiate
steps alone by placing both feet together on each step. By
three, he will walk up and down stairs with one foot on each
step just as big folks do *if he has had opportunities for
practice*. During the year he will learn to build block towers,
fill and dump containers with sand, start to use scissors (he
must have learned what "no" means first), and become
more controlled in scribbling with crayons.

Starting the year with a vocabulary of perhaps fifty
words, the child will come to his next birthday using
several hundred words. In addition to the words actually
used, there will be an understanding of most of the
vocabulary which will be used in life. At two, a child uses
words (as few as possible) to express needs or answer
questions. By three, if you have been faithful in talking to
him and listening to him, he will use fairly complete simple
sentences to share needs, problems, and feelings. Your
daughter will carry on meaningful conversations about her
world and interests if challenged and encouraged to do so.
A two-year-old will ask "What's that?" Sometimes the
asking is incessant. "Why?" will be added to the repetoire
quickly as the year proceeds. By age three, words will be
combined to ask complete questions.

The child will enjoy simple stories as the year begins,
particularly those heard often enough to be familiar. They
will be requested again and again. By the end of the year, he

can relate to you or someone else a story he knows. The ability to make up a story from a picture should also have been developed by age three (although the stories may be short, disjointed, and illogical). These stories will usually be less than 100 words long.

Storytelling ability will not develop in a vacuum. Like all other abilities, it results from stimulation and practice. It will come if you look at and discuss pictures together. "What do you see there? What else do you see? What is the dog doing? Where is the man going?" Creativity and imagination will grow as you read, discuss pictures in books, make toys together, and devise games.

Up to age 2, children have a deep interest in seeing things, feeling them, and sometimes tasting them. They can only "see" those things which are within the immediate range of their senses. During the third year, the child needs to continue to see, feel, hear, and taste things. In addition, if something is soft and yellow, he also needs to hear the words "soft" and "yellow" while seeing and feeling it. Associating the words with what he is seeing and feeling enables him to "see" and "experience" these things later in his mind when they are not where they can be perceived by his senses.

Continue fitting three-piece puzzles together. Matching games awaken and develop a lot of skills. (Match things of like color, size, and shape. Use buttons, socks, blocks, balls, etc.) Give children opportunity to string spools together.

Color sense should be developed at this age. Mention the color of everything—toys, clothes, food, etc.

Take the child for walks through the house and the neighborhood. Talk about what you see and hear.

The third year (24-36 months) is a time for shifting from emphasis on exploration, to the refining and mastering of skills. This is evident in the growing ability to use physical skills and the development of language capability. It all gets put together in the ability of the child to assume a measure of responsibility for his own care and needs. During this year children can and should be taught to do many things for themselves. It will take a lot longer, but self-confidence *and* coordination will grow as a child learns to dress himself, button his own buttons, wash his hands, and use a toothbrush. He will also learn to feed himself with a spoon and then a fork, and he will go from two-hand use of a cup to manipulating a cup or glass with one hand. Impatient parents and those whose desire to be needed is too strong can hinder the development of their children by doing too many things for them. Be careful to give lots of encouragement. Praise anything that is accomplished.

By two years your child developed a real sense of what you expect---*and* what can be expected from you in a very broad range of areas, attitudes, and actions. He will be comfortable with you *if inconsistencies in what you do and expect* do not disturb his tranquility. Your child will be ready in the coming year to assume more responsibility in the home and undertake more activity outside the home. This is also the year in which definite strides are made toward achieving specific goals in developing the character traits described in Chapter VIII.

At the start of the year, the child should be counted on to perform simple requests responsibly and consistently. (Come here---Go to your room---Bring your shoes---Put the toys in the box---Don't do that). Consistency in requiring every request to be fulfilled is essential. As the year proceeds, the child will develop the ability to do required tasks quicker and more skillfully. He will also gain the capacity to carry out two step directions. (Go to your room and take off your clothes. Put your toys in your wagon (or box) and then put the wagon (or box) into your room.)

In training your child to assume responsibility, make certain that the instructions are understood. Be sure the child has accepted the responsibility. Then see to it that responsibilities are fulfilled. This is vitally important. *Tasks and habits mastered now continue throughout life.*

MANNERS ARE IMPORTANT

During this year the foundation is laid for lifelong habits in the areas of manners, respect, etc. A child can be trained this year to respond, "Yes, ma'm" and "No, sir" when spoken to. Saying "please" and "thank you" at the appropriate times should become a part of the child's habit pattern. Boys should be encouraged to shake hands with the preacher at the end of the church service at this age. Once these "niceties" become part of a child's behavior, a little care and reinforcement will solidify them there for life.

As the child learns to say "please" and "thank you," the same attitudes toward God can be developed and expressed. During the year, parents should continue to pray with and for the child. But the child himself should also start to tell God of his needs and wants. (They will be simple and sometimes seem funny. Don't laugh though. It's very serious for a 2½ year old.) The child can and should also learn to thank the Lord for both the routine things that come from God daily---and the "specials" which have been asked for---or arrive unexpectedly.

During this third year, children will enjoy learning nursery rhymes, songs, hymns, and very simple Bible verses. For this reason, your child will be ready to move from the nursery into an actual Sunday school class at some time between twenty-four and thirty months. Make certain the Sunday school and church actually believe and teach the Bible. The Sunday school should offer a Bible class teaching facts, principles, and concepts. There should be singing with scriptural concepts. Simple Bible verses should be learned. Organized playtime in not enough.

During this period, a child's interest in nursery rhymes, songs, memorizing, etc. can be used effectively to build character while having "fun." A "nursery rhyme" with sound values is. . .

> I think it's fun to be polite,
> To say "Good morning" and "Good night",
> And "thank you, sir" and "If you please";
> There are no nicer words than these,
> Unless it is perhaps "Hello"
> Or "Sorry, I stepped on your toe."

Be careful about the "message" of some children's songs, stories, and traditional nursery rhymes. For example, some feel the traditional "Rock-a-bye baby" song may induce fears. It certainly has no positive values for a baby's life. Consider the words:

> Rock-a-bye baby on the tree top;
> When the wind blows, the cradle will rock;
> When the bough breaks, the cradle will fall, and
> Down will come baby, cradle and all.

Substitute words which drive away fear and help build a sense of security for children are:

> Jesus loves children; Jesus loves me.;
> Jesus loves you with love tenderly.
> Jesus loves all no matter how small,
> That's why I love Jesus better than all.

A series of three Christian "Mother Goose" volumes is available for families who want children to have the traditional "fun" things while being exposed to sound values and character-building concepts.

By this time a child should know that the Bible is "God's Book." During this year, start teaching your child a few simple Scripture versus or parts of verses such as:

> In the beginning God created the heaven and the earth (Genesis 1:1).

> Let us love one another (I John 4:7a).

> Be ye kind one to another (Ephesians 4:32a).

> Children obey your parents (Ephesians 6:1a).

> God is love (I John 4:8).

> The Lord our God is one Lord (Deuteronomy 6:4b).

While memorizing the verses, explain the concepts which they contain. Start integrating these principles into what is required of the child.

SUMMING IT UP

Give your children opportunities to develop and grow. But do not panic if your child is not on the exact schedule of a neighbor child or a cousin. Do not feel you and your child are failures if he does not conform to the latest schedule in a book or magazine. The authors of the *Games to Grow On* material which was mentioned earlier, so wisely caution:

> All children go through certain stages of development in basically the same order. However, each child arrives at these stages on his own timetable. . .Your child should not be rushed or pushed to arrive at a stage early—but should be provided with experiences which will help him develop to his fullest at each step along the way. . .Remember, all apples on a tree do not ripen at the same time.

   Play with your child, enjoy him, and give him experiences to grow on. But, remember also that he needs time just to find things out for himself. Do not fall into the trap of over-organizing your child and your life.

CHAPTER VI

1.   Dr. Warren Brown, *Growing Up - The Early Years,* Copyright (undated) Ferguson-Florissant School District, Ferguson MO 63135
2.   Ibid.
3.   Koch, *Total Baby Development,* Copyright 1976, Wyden Books
4.   *Games To Grow On,* Copyright (undated), Ferguson-Florissant School District, Ferguson MO 63135
5.   Hyles, *How To Rear Infants,* Copyright 1979, Hyles Anderson Publishers, Hammond IN
6.   Koch, *Total Baby Development,* pg. 3 & 21.
7.   Washington *Times,* Oct 11, 1983
8.   St. Louis *Globe Democrat,* Mar 4-5, 1978.

Chapter VII

GETTING READY FOR SCHOOL AND LIFE

Whom shall he teach knowledge? and whom shall he make to understand doctrine? them that are weaned from the milk, and drawn from the breasts. For precept must be upon precept, precept upon precept; line upon line, line upon line; here a little, and there a little.

--Isaiah 28:9-10

EVEN THOUGH THE PROGRESS WILL BE LESS DRAMATIC, the next twenty-four months will be very important. You will be getting your son or daughter ready for school and life. The time will pass rapidly. A host of additional skills still need to be developed and mastered. Present skills need to be refined and reinforced. Mature attitudes need to be fostered. If you have been doing your job faithfully, a good foundation has been solidly laid. To be fully ready for a kindergarten with a well-rounded academic program, your child will need to acquire certain minimum skills in the next two years: They include the ability to:

. . .care for his own toilet needs.

. . .be able to take care of his outer clothing, scarf, mittens, boots and snowpants without assistance except in very difficult situations.

. . .be able to go up and down steps with one foot on each step.

. . .know how to use cleansing tissue properly and cover his mouth when coughing or sneezing.

. . .be willing to be away from home for six hours without concern. (Treat this as a normal thing and give the child some oppportunities to grow into the experience as the time draws nearer.)

...be free from baby talk and be able to carry on a conversation quite freely with an adult apart from family.

...be able to keep fingers and objects out of his mouth.

...know how to listen to, actually hear and then follow simple two and three step directions.

...be able to relate a sequence of events in order.

...be able to handle pencils, crayons, and scissors comfortably.

...have an interest in books, stories, numbers and music. (Ability to read, write, or do math is not necessary.)

...be willing to obey the teacher or whoever is in charge.

Getting ready for school will require continued growth and development in four basic areas during the next two years. These include (1) the development of certain physical skills and abilities, (2) mental development particularly in the areas of language skills and awareness of the world in which he lives, (3) emotional and social growth and (4) a broadening of spiritual horizons.

PHYSICAL DEVELOPMENT

More important than how much or how little your child grows at this stage is how he improves in the ability to use his body. As the child exercises, plays, runs, goes up and down stairs, and carries things, needed large-muscle development will continue.

Development and control of small muscles is the major need during the fourth and fifth years. Children must have opportunities to color, paint, write, dress themselves, button clothing, open and close snaps, tie shoes, and manipulate all sorts of gadgets and things.

Dr. Ruth Beechick, children's editor for the Accent Sunday school literature and Bible curriculum, in her book, *Teaching Preschoolers,[1]* gives an important observation concerning physical development at the start of the thirty-six to sixty month age period:

> At this age, children have developed some precision with large muscle movements (walking, running, etc.), however. . .he is not at the same stage in small movements, such as those required for writing and coloring. This is why it is inappropriate for us to require precision in this kind of work. These are skills which depend more on maturation than on learning. When the time is right the child will learn these things easily.

She also gives an important insight into a child's
interests which can be helpful to parents as well as the
preschool teachers to whom she is writing. She says:

> A characteristic of this period is that the child indulges in new
> abilities for their own sake. When using paints, crayons, or
> clay. . .The motion—the manipulating itself—is the purpose of
> the activity.

> This is sometimes hard for teachers to adjust to, since our adult
> view is so oriented toward the finished product. We think the
> purpose of classroom activity is to make something, to
> complete a picture, to model a recognizable object of some other
> end product. But the child view is oriented toward the process.
> He is painting or coloring or smashing. He is sweeping the
> brush or pushing the crayon or poking the clay. Only gradually
> does he become interested in making "things." *The child needs
> plenty of experience with process before centering on the end
> product.* Do not force this stage before its time.

During the period from two to four years of age, a child's
"art" abilities and interests progress through three stages.
They are:

1. Scribble stage. Exploratory manipulation of muscles and
crayon or pencil.

2. Recognition stage. Child "sees" something in his scribbles.

3. Representational stage. Child can name what he will draw
before drawing it.

Children usually reach the representational stage at
about age four. In the early stages of representational
drawing, parents sometimes need a good imagination to
"see" that the child has accomplished what he announced
he would do.

GROWING MENTAL ABILITIES

Your child's vocabulary (about 150 words at twenty-four
months) will increase tenfold by age four. But it will happen
day by day. By the fourth birthday, the child will be using
1500 words. To achieve this goal, children need to be talked
to, questioned, listened to, and read to regularly.* As

----

* Restudying the section on "It Takes Time To Read" in chapter 3 would
be helpful now.

vocabulary grows they should be required to speak distinctly and clearly. Poor pronunciation, sloppy grammar and slang terms should be corrected. Efforts to develop good speech patterns are a mark of your care, concern and love. Your diligence will show your child that "doing right" in all things, including speaking, is important. Requiring a child to "say it right" every time may seem to be nitpicking. Overlooking "small" errors is an easy way out at the time but will permit bad habits to develop which may take years to correct.

If you want your children to have the confidence and assurance in life which comes with speaking correctly, make sure they start right. You need to speak correctly in their presence. Make the effort to polish and refine grammar, pronunciation, and manners. *Be sure to spend as much time (or more) praising and rewarding right actions and achievements as you do correcting errors.*

During the 36-48 month period, a sense of time starts to develop. Concepts of past, present and future begin to form and are expressed. Time concepts broaden and deepen. By age five, a child should know what day it is, be able to name the days of the week, and have an awareness of what day follows Sunday. He will be interested in calendars and clocks. He cannot tell time yet. He will be interested in finding birthdays and holidays on the calendar.

An awareness of numbers begins to develop at about thirty-six months. By age four, the child can count three objects. In another six months he can count to ten. By the time he starts to kindergarten he may be able to count to twenty-five, write a few numbers, and tell how many fingers are held up on a hand. Being able to count by rote comes long before the child can tell whether there are three or five or seven objects in a display.

Interest in the ABC's will also begin to develop. Keep in mind that the sounds a letter makes are more important than the letter's name in learning to read. Therefore, when your child starts showing an interest in letters, it is perhaps more important for him to think of the sound a "b" makes rather than the name of the letter. Naturally, he will first master the names of the letters. As he does, start developing interest in what the letter "says."

Games with flash cards are of interest and help---if not

overdone. Flash card games should start with pictures and
proceed to numbers, letters, etc. Ruth Beechick tells how to
make and use card games. She says:

> One of the most flexible teaching devices you can have is a set
> of cards pertaining to whatever topic you wish to teach. . .An
> easy-to-make set could have pictures of things God made.
> Collect pictures to paste on your cards or draw simple pictures
> of things God made—flower, tree, bird, sun, moon, stars, and
> other objects.

A variety of games can be played with such cards. Start
by having children name what is pictured as cards are held
up. Once a child becomes acquainted with the things
pictured, a variation is to have him name a "thing" God
makes and "win" a card picturing that object or thing.   In
this way, the child is stimulated to form mental pictures of
things which are not actually in view. To get further
variety, place cards on the floor face up in full view of the
child. Then ask, "Can you bring me the picture showing
where birds build their nests?" Another time the child
might be asked to bring the same card by asking, "Bring
the one that has leaves." For a very young child, the first
step might be, "Bring the tree." Other variations can be
developed. Display just three or four cards. Then turn them
face down and remove one. Let the child turn all of the cards
over and tell which one is missing.

A variety of card sets can be made picturing Christmas
and Easter words and happenings, animals, various types
of people, etc. During the latter part of the four-to-five-year
age time, flash cards with letters, numbers, etc. can be used.
Children who are interested can be exposed not only to
letter names but also to their sounds as well.

GROWING SPIRITUALLY

Continue to broaden spiritual horizons through your
example and by exposing the child to the Word of God. As
you do, the child's knowledge of God and care for others will
deepen. Continued effort and diligence are also needed to
develop the character traits described in the next chapter.

Daily Bible reading and prayer should be a consistent
part of your child's schedule. Read, tell and discuss
children's Bible stories. Use stories about how God involves
Himself in the lives of people. Such stories help children to

see God as a person. Continually emphasize God's love and care and provision and protection. Specific actions which will broaden your child's love and respect for the Lord are included in the character traits section in the next chapter.

Children at this age love to memorize. During the three-to-four-year age period have children memorize such verses as:

> All we like sheep have gone astray; we have turned everyone to his own way (Isaiah 53:6a & b). (Memorize in two sections).
>
> I am the good shepherd (John 10:11a).
>
> The Lord our God is one Lord (Deuteronomy 6:4).
>
> Thou shalt not kill (Exodus 20:13). (Explain that hurting is the first step toward killing.)
>
> Thou shalt not steal. (Exodus 20:15).

Use care to explain and make the teachings of the verses personal. Between the fourth and fifth birthdays, a child should regularly review verses learned earlier and add to them. Additional verses to be mastered during this time are:

> Children, obey your parents in the Lord: for this is right (Ephesians 6:1).
>
> Honour thy father and mother; which is the first commandment with promise; That it may be well with thee, and thou mayest live long on the earth (Ephesians 6:2-3). (Work to memorize this and other verses in about 3 sections adding an additional section as one is mastered.)
>
> Speak every man truth with his neighbor (Ephesians 4:25).
>
> Give, and it shall be given unto you (Luke 6:38a).
>
> Let no corrupt communication proceed out of your mouth (Ephesians 4:29).
>
> All we like sheep have gone astray; we have turned every one to his own way; and the Lord hath laid on him the iniquity of us all (Isaiah 53:6).
>
> I am the good shepherd; the good shepherd giveth his life for the sheep (John 10:11).
>
> For God so loved the world, that he gave his only begotten Son, that whosoever believeth in him should not perish but have everlasting life (John 3:16). (Memorize in two or three sections).
>
> Train up a child in the way he should go: and when he is old, he will not depart from it (Proverbs 22:6).

Christ died for our sins according to the scriptures. . .And that he was buried, and that he arose again the third day according to the scriptures. (I Corinthians 15:3b-4).

Why seek ye the living among the dead? He is not here but is risen (Luke 24:5b-6a).

If your child shows real interest and ability at memorizing, Bible Memory Association, P. O. Box 12000, Ringgold, LA 71068, supplies a colorful picture book guide for Scripture memorization for preschoolers. Titled *The ABC Memory Plan*, the book covers three stages of work for ages three to six. The child learns verses and the ABC's at the same time. The cost is $5.00.

SOCIAL AND EMOTIONAL DEVELOPMENT

During the third and fourth years, your child will go through periods of being a cheerful, outgoing, social little boy or girl. He or she will also have periods of withdrawal, shyness, insecurity and/or rebellion and stubbornness. The "experts" disagree on whether these ups and downs are necessary and normal. They also disagree about when the various cycles appear. The "down" periods may come at times when the child is on the verge of making a breakthrough into some new area of accomplishment, attitude, or outlook. Some ups and downs are normal. However, a conscientious parent must guard against brushing aside symptoms of a real problem with a reassuring, "It's just a stage. He'll get over it in time."

The ups and downs should be the occasion for a careful inventory. Is the child facing changing demands which have him under pressure? All pressure is not bad. Without some pressure there is no progress. However, expecting more from a child than he is capable of producing at any stage of growth can be destructive. Could a change in your schedule or attitude have triggered the change in your child's outlook, attitude, or behavior? (Arrival of a new baby, a move, or changing churches, all have effects.) Could some new friend be having an influence?

As a child shows evidence of going through a stage, it is important to pray. Ask for God's wisdom in diagnosing and handling the problem. As you pray, be sensitive to what God may want to show you about your own spiritual condition. Sin and spiritual problems in the lives of parents can be reflected in a child's behavior.

When stages develop (at whatever age) do not panic. Surround the child with love and understanding while seeking the cause and cure. Maintain established rules and standards of behavior and conduct. This is important. The "stage" may be just a periodic testing of your authority and determination to maintain control. If so, deal with it firmly. Most important avoid the temptation to learn to live with and accept substandard behavior.

GETTING IT ALL IN PLACE (36-60 months)

There is so much to teach a child in getting him ready for school and life. There are skills to develop and abilities to awaken. Habits need to be formed. Interests in the world and all that is in it need to be stimulated. A talented young mother has developed a concept which can be helpful in putting it all together during the last years before school starts.

Jeanne Hanson is the mother of two children. Since her children were very small, she has disciplined herself to spend ten minutes a day in actual, planned teaching situations with each child. The ten minutes is divided into two five-minute sessions.

The mini-school time is spent playing learning games with the child. Mrs. Hanson has recorded her experiences in a book, *Game Plans for Children: Raising A Brighter Child In 10 Minutes A Day*. She describes the structured, planned setting for parent-taught mini-school this way:

> The "teacher" should give his or her child undivided attention. Set up a table and two chairs in the same room every day—shut the door. If you're especially efficient, you can even start school at the same time every day so your child expects it. It's worthwhile, too, to make sure that your other child's or children's needs are taken care of ahead of time so that you won't be interrupted.

Her approach to discipline is described this way:

> Mini-school can also serve as a good preparation for the rules of school later when children have to "do what the teacher says."

Mrs. Hanson's book gives hundreds of ideas she has developed for learning games. There are games which introduce children to the world. Attention is given to the things in the world and their names, their functions and characteristics. There are games which develop the senses. Others help to coordinate eye-hand movements or small muscle development. These are skills which will be used when a child learns to write. There are games which emphasize recognition of colors, sizes, shapes, opposites, similarities, differences, etc. As children reach age four, reading readiness games which help in learning letter sounds are introduced.

Home tasks and responsibilities are on the mini-school curriculum. At a very young age, children are taught to set the table. In the process, the child learns right from left and how to count out knives, forks, and spoons for each family member. Children are taught how to pour liquids, water plants, empty wastebaskets, and a myriad of other household tasks. Lessons in mini-school prepare children to make their own beds by age five.

There are lessons on how to answer the telephone properly. Using the phone to make calls comes later. Rules for good manners and the reasons for the rules are in the "curriculum."

The hows and whys of how toilets flush, vacuum cleaners work, stoves cook, lights light, cars run, and washing machines wash are interesting and important.

Mini-school exercises include memorizing such basic and needed facts as the days of the week, the months of the year, the four seasons, and the time of various holidays.

The mini-school teaches the things children should know and need to do. All parents would agree that children need to be taught the concepts in the "curriculum." Many would be learned just in the process of "growing up." Some would be missed, however. The structure and the discipline imposed on parents by the mini-school concept forces mom and dad to consciously decide what needs to be learned—and how to teach it. Once the lessons have been taught (and retaught and reviewed again and again) the parent is more likely to make the child accountable for performing what has been learned. Subject matter is varied from day to day and week by week.

As children start to regular school the mini-school continues. Its sessions reinforce, support, supplement and enrich what the child learns during the regular school day. By the time a child starts to "real school" he has already had over 1200 mini-school sessions. The two five-minute daily sessions do not put too much pressure on the child. Yet, they insure that a parent works in a systematic way to develop and teach needed abilities, skills, attitudes, and perception. In doing it, the parent spends a brief but definite time alone with each child daily. Mini-school can be a fun time (learning can be fun—although sometimes it is just hard work). Children look forward to it. It helps to build openness and communications between parent and child. Parents get needed insights into the basic abilities, interests, limitations, and needs of their children.

The "mini-school" concept is summarized this way. Mrs. Hanson writes:

> Ten minutes a day may not sound like much time. It certainly does not create an overemphasis on school skills and creativity at the expense of play or other activities. But just think—ten minutes is a long time if you spend it staring out a window, kissing or running at top speed. It is surely a long time from the perspective of a young child. And it can be plenty of time, too, if you regularly spend five minutes of it in a planned learning game session with your child and another five minutes in a creativity session. Many days the time will fly by. But even on days when it doesn't seem to, it is still manageable.

Using the mini-school structure may help parents continually to consider what needs to be taught. It can discipline them to do the needed teaching. By age two or three the structured, scheduled, daily "class" session can be helpful. Once the child reaches age three a lot of skills, abilities, and concepts need to be imparted to get a child ready for school in two short years. There are many responsibilities a child needs to start assuming for himself and as a part of the family. Mini-school can teach many of these needed skills.

In her book Mrs. Hanson does not try to create the impression that being a good parent can be accomplished in ten minutes a day. She says:

> The (mini-school) plan covers school preparation skills and creativity quite well, but it is absolutely not a blueprint for spending a total of only ten minutes a day with your child. It is not a method for fast toilet training, nor is it a shortcut to artistic expression, a provision for physical exercise or a quick way of teaching moral values. Neither does it encompass

reading to your child, cuddling, taking educational walks, and trips, talking about feelings or stopping to smell daisies. All of these are very important and need to be done in addition to the plan presented here.

Mini-school is just a starting place. Wise parents are alert to recognize and constantly use opportunities to share life-building experiences with children. A man who has successfully challenged and trained hundreds of thousands of people during the last twenty years emphasizes the importance of looking for God-given teaching opportunities in the home. The founder of the *Institute in Basic Youth Conflicts,* Bill Gothard, says:

> God's educational objectives were designed to be carried out in the home long before anyone thought about a school. The school can be an effective extension of the home but can never take its place.

> Educators realize that the most effective learning is achieved in living experiences rather than classroom theory. The difficulty has come in that parents often do not have the alertness or ability to turn everyday situations into teaching experiences. Neither do they have a well thought out body of content which must be communicated to each child at different levels of maturity.[3]

For these reasons parents too often delegate their teaching responsibility to others---the school, church, etc. Suggestions for returning the home to its rightful place in the overall education scheme include:

> Continually recognize home situations which can be turned into vital learning experiences. Most parents would be amazed at the vast and varied amount of learning which is possible by using opportunities as they come.

> Recognize that God does not expect parents to design a curriculum but rather to share with children what God is teaching the parents from Scripture and life.

> Discover and rechannel the interest and motivation of each child for learning by listening and asking questions. Their answers will help us understand what children are seeing and feeling. In the process we help them define and reinforce God's goals for their lives and create in them the curiosity which will cause them to receive vital information.

Conversations and discussions at mealtimes are good times for the family to examine important life concepts and truths. Bill Gothard says:

> Carefully planned questions, illustrations and stories which
> are casually but appropriately shared by the father during a
> mealtime discussion will provide the daily exhortation so
> necessary in each life.

Mealtime discussions should start when children are
very small. Continued through life, they are important
times for building principles and attitudes into children
about life, the world, current events, etc. These sessions can
also help stimulate a child's thinking process, imagination,
and ability to express himself.

As important as it is to prepare your child for school and
life, do not go overboard. The need for a balanced approach
cannot be over-emphasized. God says:

> To every thing there is a season, and a time to every purpose
> under the heaven (Ecclesiastes 3:1).

Be sensitive to when your child is ready to learn new
skills and be stimulated to undertake new challenges. If
you can avoid the temptation to pressure Johnny or Susan
to keep up with a cousin or the neighbor's child, learning
can be fascinating and fun for your child and you. Just be
careful to provide exposure to proper growing experiences,
ideas, and concepts.

THE BIG DAY APPROACHES

Before you realize it, your child will be ready for
kindergarten. If you have followed the suggestions in this
book, your son or daughter will succeed and perhaps excel
in whatever kindergarten you select. If you have been
working to give your child spiritual awareness and to
develop his character, he will be happiest and challenged
most effectively in a Christian school. Christian schools
emphasize character development. Discipline standards
similar to those you require at home will be maintained at
school.

Public schools generally reflect the standards and values
of the communities which operate them. As the moral
values of American society have deteriorated drastically
since 1960, schools have encountered similar problems.
These problems have caused concerned parents to look for
an alternative means of fulfilling their God-given respon-

sibility to educate their children.

Christian schools have been established in recent years as ministries of Bible-believing churches. Teachers are born-again Christians. Good standards of conduct, dress, and appearance are maintained. They emphasize fair, firm discipline, love of country, and character development. Academically, students in Christian schools generally average one to two years above national averages on standardized achievement tests.

The standards of discipline and academic excellence in a Christian school are important. However, the real motivation for enrolling a child in a Christian school was stated best by a wise and conscientious black mother a few years ago. Asked on the application blank to state why she desired to enroll her child in a Christian school, she said. . .

> . . .because we want our daughter to have the same standards, values and teaching in school that she receives at home and in church.

DON'T STOP NOW

Rearing children is a life-long responsibility (and joy). The principles and practices developed and used during the first five years should be continued (with modifications required as children get older). The responsibility of child rearing will not even end when your children are grown. The Bible requires that after we learn and apply God's principles for living in our own lives, that we are to. . .

> . . .teach them thy sons, and thy sons' sons. . .that they may teach their children (Deuteronomy 4:9-10).

Chapter VII

1. Beechick, *Teaching Preschoolers,* Copyright 1979, Accent Publishers, Denver, CO
2. Hanson, *Game Plans For Children*, Copyright 1981, G. P. Putnam Sons, New York
3. Gothard, *Character Sketches,* Vol. I, Copyright 1976, Institute of Basic Youth Conflicts, Oakbrook, IL

Chapter VIII

CHARACTER IS THE KEY

*The integrity of the upright shall guide them; but the
perverseness of transgressors shall destroy them.*
                                              — *Proverbs 11:3*

ABOUT A DOZEN VERY BASIC TRAITS must be
formed into a child's character before he starts to school. If
these basic character traits are lacking, the child is
seriously handicapped in school and throughout life.
Character is essential no matter how intelligent and
talented a child may be.

Amazingly, a careful study of historical records shows
that the needed traits are the very characteristics that the
parents of George Washington and John Wesley developed
in their sons 250 years ago. These basic character traits,
supplemented by several dozen others Washington and
Wesley developed as they grew older, made the two men the
giants of their age.

Qualities acquired early in life by both Washington and
Wesley and needed by your child include:

1.	Attentiveness	8.	Faith
2.	Obedience	9.	Truthfulness
3.	Contentment	10.	A sense of security
4.	Neatness	11.	Meekness
5.	Reverence	12.	Cautiousness
6.	Forgiveness	13.	Patience
7.	Gratefulness		

These characteristics are essential if a child is to have a
good relationship with his parents, the teacher in school,
and his employer on the job. They are vital for success in
marriage. They are the foundations upon which the
maturing person will add another thirty or so important

character traits later in life. Character also provides the foundation the child needs in order to develop and maintain a good personal relationship with the Lord Jesus Christ after salvation.

Character does not develop spontaneously. It must be woven into the fabric of the child's being by dedicated parents. To develop character in children, parents must know what they want to achieve. Then they can learn how to accomplish their goals. The job is actually a simple one for parents who combine dedication with some old-fashioned common sense. Anyone can do it who keeps the goal in mind and follows through on a day-to-day basis.

The goal is to produce a disciplined life for the child. Having a disciplined life causes a child . . .

> . . . to do the right thing, in the right way, at the right time, with the right attitude even when he or she doesn't want to.

A disciplined life is produced initially through control by parents, teachers, and other external authorities. Children have to be taught to do what is right—and made to do it. The ultimate goal is to have the child discipline himself through means of his own character.

Character is . . .

> . . . recognizing that which is right, kind, decent, wise and loving in every situation; having the desire to do these things; and acting consistently in accordance with this knowlege and desire.

A well-known Christian educator, Dr. Ron Brooks of Greenville, S.C., defines character most simply as . . .

> . . . doing right even when you don't feel like it.

The Bible never uses the word *character*. However, the words *integrity* in the Old Testament and *virtue* in the New Testament have the same basic meaning. The importance of character is shown by Proverbs 11:3 which says:

> The integrity of the upright shall guide them; but the perverseness of transgressors shall destroy them.

Having integrity will enable a person to control himself and do right even under pressure or in times of crisis. The Hebrew word which is translated *integrity* in the Old

Testament basically means "to live uprightly." It also carries the ideal of a person who is the same all the way through. Integrity or character is not just something done on the outside for show. A person of character has inner convictions which control outward behavior. God, recognized the importance of integrity when He told Satan that in spite of all Job's troubles . . .

> . . . still he holdeth fast his integrity, although thou movedst me against him, to destroy him without cause (Job 2:3).

Job never quit trusting God and doing right even when his family, his possessions, and his health had been taken away from him. He had integrity (or character). He continued to do right because it was right to do right. That is character!

The world needs people of character. One of the world's most prestigious accounting firms regularly hires many graduates of a leading fundamental Christian university even though it is not "accredited." They are not hired just because they have had fine business training but because they have character. Talent and ability mean little without the character to use it right. Dick Vermiel coached the Philadelphia Eagles to the Super Bowl a few years ago. Afterwards he said that on the football field character is more important than talent. The person of character stays with the job---finishes the task---does it right---gives his best *all the time.*

Dr. Jack Hyles tells how to develop character. To build character, he says, you must . . .

> . . . discipline yourself to do right until it becomes such a part of you that you do right by reflex.

A saved person has God living in him. Discipline and character let God manifest His presence and power continually in and through the person's life. *This is the only real basis for a happy, successful life.* Look at it this way. When we decide to do right, God can show His life and power through us. When we decide to do wrong---or just drift down the wrong path---God who is in us will not show or release His power. God will not be involved in wrongdoing.

Developing a child's character is not a two or three step process. It is not accomplished in a few weeks or months like learning to walk, throwing a ball, putting on socks, saying simple words, or other physical or mental achievements.

Developing a child's character starts at birth. It continues through life. To develop a child's character, parents need to understand which character traits are important and necessary. They must constantly be aware of their absence in any situation as the child grows. Parents have difficulty spotting a deficiency in a child's life when they have the same shortcoming. Therefore parents who get serious about building character into the lives of their children, frequently have to do a major job of rehabilitation on themselves.

Basic traits a child needs before starting school include:

ATTENTIVENESS

Attentiveness is the trait of listening carefully to everyone who speaks. The attentive person also notices when others need help. Being attentive causes a person to be alert to those from whom he can learn, get help, or be warned.

To know whether the person speaking is an authority who should be obeyed, one who has a need, or someone who can help in some way, an individual must develop the practice of listening carefully to everyone. The degree of attentiveness a person gives to others shows his evaluation of their worth and importance.

Attentiveness is an absolute necessity for learning obedience and safety. Attentiveness is the first of the major character traits which need to be developed in a child or any individual.

The child who comes to the kindergarten classroom at age five without having acquired the trait of attentiveness will be seriously handicapped in many ways. If he does not listen to instructions he cannot follow them. If he does not listen to the material as it is taught, he will not learn. A child who has never learned to listen when spoken to may be diagnosed by school authorities as "learning disabled." A child who is not attentive may not hear the warning which can save his life. A child must develop attentiveness if he is to be sensitive later in life to the promptings, restraints and "still small voice" of God's Holy Spirit.

God commands us to be attentive. In Hebrews 2:1 we read:

> Therefore we ought to give the more earnest heed to the things which we have heard, lest at any time we should let them slip.

A child who from infancy has been regularly talked to, played with, and disciplined will learn to listen and become attentive. A child who is rarely talked to personally will learn not to listen because the voices that talk have no significance for him.

To develop attentiveness fully, children should be required to stop whatever they are doing immediately whenever they are spoken to. They should be trained then to look directly at the person speaking. When the child is between twenty-four and thirty months old, he can also be trained to respond "Yes, sir" or "Yes, M'am" when spoken to. This builds attentiveness, prepares the way for obedience, and helps instill respect in the child.

Parents can show that they want their child to be attentive and can help to develop the trait by regularly asking, "Now, what did I say?" or "Tell me what I asked you to do." Fun games can be developed where the child repeats two, three or four words in sequence or instructions for a series of sequential actions.

Once children learn to listen when spoken to, they are ready to learn to obey. Attention is vital. There can be no obedience without attentiveness.

OBEDIENCE

Obedience is doing what those in authority request or want. It is the opposite of "doing your own thing." True obedience involves doing what an authority wants immediately, respectfully, joyfully, and completely. Obedience requires the submission of the will of the individual to those in charge. True obedience ultimately stems from submission to God. It is God who commands obedience to parents, governmental authorities, the pastor, the boss on the job, and those to whom these authorities delegate their authority.

"Obey" is the most important single word in the Bible. Being obedient is the key to receiving all of God's blessings. To be saved from sin and hell, a person must *obey* God's command, "Believe on the Lord Jesus Christ, and thou shalt be saved" (Acts 16:31). To get the new life God promises as a part of salvation, the individual must be willing to *obey* the command of the Lord Jesus, who said, "Ye must be born again" (John 3:3).

To enjoy the fullness of the Spirit and the life of love, joy, peace, patience, gentleness, goodness, meekness, faith, and temperance which goes with it, we must *obey*. The Bible says that God gives the Holy Spirit to "them that *obey* Him" (Acts 5:32).

Financial freedom comes from obeying God. He says:

> Bring ye all the tithes into the store house, that there may be meat in mine house, and prove me now herewith, saith the Lord of hosts, if I will not open you the windows of heaven, and pour you out a blessing, that there shall not be room enough to receive it (Malachi 3:10).

There are a multitude of other material and spiritual blessings for those who *obey* God. Among them is long life. Ephesians 6:1-3 commands:

> Children, *obey* your parents in the Lord: for this is right. Honour thy father and mother; which is the first commandment with promise; That it may be well with thee, *and thou mayest live long on the earth.*

Obedience to God and all His authorities must start in the home. No one wants to obey. All are rebels by nature. No parent ever needs to teach children to disobey. It comes naturally. Rebellion and disobedience come from the nature man got in the Garden of Eden when Adam and Eve rebelled against God. Every person born since has been a rebel. The Bible says, "God created man in the likeness of God." When creation was finished, "God saw every thing that He had made, and, behold it was very good" (Genesis 1:31). Obviously, something has happened since. The "something" was Adam's sin. He rebelled against God. He became a sinner by actions and by nature. Since then, all men have been born with Adam's sinful image rather than being born in the image of God. Genesis 5:3 says:

> And Adam lived an hundred and thirty years, and begat a son *in his own likeness, after his image;* and called his name Seth.

Seth had a son "after his image." Everyone since has had children born "in their own image." They have all been sinners. The first word most children use is "No!" It is expressed either with the mouth or with a shake of the head.

The child who never has to obey in the home will develop into an unhappy rebel who will have serious difficulties throughout life. There will be problems in school, in obeying laws, and in submitting to God's Word and the leading of His Holy Spirit. The boy who has not learned to obey at home when young will always be unhappy on the job. The little girl who has not developed an obedient heart in childhood will have great difficulty fulfilling her God-given role in marriage years later.

As important as obedience is, no one is obedient by nature. Obedience comes as a result of training. The child-training process outlined in Chapters III and VI are essential to developing an obedient child.

Until the child submits to the control of parents, teachers, other authorities, and God he will never see their love. As long as a person is struggling with an authority, he can see only what the authority is denying or trying to take away or requiring. Once there is submission, the authority's love and wisdom can be seen. The protection which comes from being under authority can then also be enjoyed. Through constant training, the submitted child can learn to obey immediately, completely *and cheerfully*.

Obedient children are happy children. They are secure because they know their limits. Disobedient children are unhappy children. (Their parents are unhappy also.) II Corinthians 10:5 shows the ultimate goal in developing obedience in a child. The Bible says:

> Casting down imaginations, and every high thing that exalteth itself against the knowledge of God, *and bringing into captivity every thought to the obedience of Christ.*

Parents who have difficulty training children to obey should make a careful check as to whether they have a right attitude toward the authority of their own parents, employer, the law, and God. No one can be a channel for authority unless under authority personally. Even the Lord Jesus was a model of obedience when He was here on earth. He obeyed Joseph and His mother even when He knew better than they what He was here to do. (See Luke 2:41-52.) Not only was He subject to Mary and Joseph, the scriptures show that He also always obeyed and sought to please His heavenly Father. In John 8:28b-29, He said:

> ... I do nothing of myself; but as my Father hath taught me, I speak these things. And he that hath sent me is with me: the Father hath not left me alone; *for I do always those things that please Him.*

CONTENTMENT

Because the first woman, Eve, was not content with all that God had given her to enjoy in the Garden of Eden, she ate of the forbidden fruit. Since that time, discontent (not being satisfied with what we have) and covetousness (wanting what we do not have or what others do have) have plagued the human race.

Covetousness keeps us from really enjoying what we do have—no matter how much it might be. A multi-millionaire was reportedly asked, "Mr. Blank, how many millions do you think it would take to satisfy you?" The very wealthy man is reported to have thought for just an instant before replying, "At least one more million than I will ever have." He knew himself—and the entire human race.

A gigantic industry invests billions of dollars every year promoting dissatisfaction. Hundreds of thousands of very talented people devote themselves to making us dissatisfied with what we have. They dedicate themselves to inducing covetousness in us. This is called advertising. The advertiser uses radio, TV, the newspapers, billboards, and direct mail. Some advertising is informative and helpful. Most of it is cleverly and effectively designed to stimulate desires for things we do not have. Pictures, words, music and color are skillfully combined to make us get a bigger, better, newer, and fancier model of what we already have.

If children are going to be pleasant companions and grow up to be happy themselves, they must develop the character trait of contentment. Contentment must be developed. It has to be learned. The Apostle Paul said:

> I have *learned,* in whatsoever state I am, therewith to be content (Philippians 4:11b)

Every parent needs to help his children learn to be content. In doing so, parents should always insure that a baby has what it really needs. Be sensitive to a child's need for increased food, warm clothing, and love. In other words, do not foster discontent by withholding or neglecting real needs. The Bible makes this very clear. I Timothy 5:8 says:

> But if any provide not for his own [relatives], and especially for those of his own house, he hath denied the faith, and is worse than an infidel.

To teach a child to be content—to help him to learn contentment—there are a number of steps to take and policies to enforce. They include:

> Children must learn to eat what is served to them—or go hungry. They must learn that what you provide will satisfy and nourish them. If the parent ever substitutes "goodies" because a child expresses dissatisfaction with what has been served, the fires of dissatisfaction will soon be raging in many areas of life. Ultimately, any unsatisfied want will produce tantrums.

> Children should be taught to finish what they start. The boring task, the hard task, the seemingly impossible task cannot be abandoned because something more interesting or different or easier becomes available.

> Children who are required to play with their own toys rather than hollering for (or taking) the playthings of others will learn to be content with what they have. To develop contentment, children must learn that displays of dissatisfaction and covetousness *never* bring results.

Children should be taught at an early age to amuse themselves *by creating rather than by getting*. Games children invent themselves using available clothes pins, rubber bands, etc. will keep them busy and happy longer than new things. A "new" toy quickly becomes "old." Developing a creative mind in even one child enables any number of children (three, five, or fifteen) to invent a workable set of rules for a pickup baseball game which can keep them busy and happy for days on end. Children do not have to be programmed into a constant stream of Boy or Girl Scouts, Little League, or dancing lessons to be content.

Children should not be allowed to see too much. The Bible teaches that we become discontent through what we see. King David, one of God's real giants, fell into awful sin because He looked. II Samuel 11:2 says:

> And it came to pass in an eveningtide, that David arose from off his bed, and walked upon the roof of the king's house: and from the roof *he saw* a woman washing herself; and the woman

was very beautiful *to look upon.*

David looked and David wanted. His looking led to discontent with his own wife. He took Bathsheba and she conceived a child. Her husband was away at the time fighting in David's army. To try to cover his sin, David finally had the husband placed in the hottest point of the battle where he was killed. It all started with *seeing* and then *looking* covetously.

This is not an isolated instance. Seeing and looking at things that God said Israel shouldn't have led another Old Testament man into deep sin. He and his family were ultimately destroyed because of his actions. After Achan's sin was exposed, Joshua 7:20-21 records this explanation:

> And Achan answered Joshua, and said, Indeed I have sinned against the Lord God of Israel, and thus and thus have I done: When *I saw* among the spoils a goodly Babylonish garment, and two hundred shekels of silver, and a wedge of gold of fifty shekels weight, then *I coveted* them, and *took* them; and, behold, they are hid in the earth in the midst of my tent, and the silver under it.

He *saw*---he *coveted*---he *took*. All Israel suffered defeat in battle because of his sin and disobedience. He and his family were executed for his crime. Achan became discontented with what God had provided when *he saw* other things. We need to be careful to protect our children from seeing too much.

Shoplifting, robbery, car thefts, and adultery all start with the discontent that comes from seeing too much. TV commercials are designed with the express purpose of building discontent with present possessions. The TV causes covetousness (the desire for something new or different). Children who watch TV will have all sorts of "wants" programmed into their minds which will surface in the supermarket or other stores.

Window shopping by children (or adults) is very unwise. It wastes time. Window shopping also promotes discontent and covetousness. Parents should not window shop themselves. They should not expose their children to experiences which promote covetousness and discontent either. Shopping trips should be planned to buy those things which the family needs---and can afford. Shopping together as a family can provide important learning experiences but safeguard against promoting covetousness.

Carefully control the kind of friendships your children build even at a very early age. Avoid close relationships with children whose parents try to show love by giving in to every wish and whim and demand of the child. Protect your children from close exposure to families who substitute things for love.

To protect your children from discontent, never let an "I wish" go unanswered. Sometimes the child can be shown how he or she can get whatever is wanted through work or by making the toy or game. In other instances, take the time to show children they do not really need the thing they wished for. Sometimes children need to be brought to an understanding that they are not yet ready to use or enjoy whatever they are coveting. Finally, a child should be made aware that God will provide the desired item or condition when the time is right. Children can be taught to pray for what they want. When God provides the desired (and prayed for) item, parents should be sure the child recognizes and acknowledges what God has done.

The real key to contentment in life stems from the knowledge that God is in total and absolute control of all things, that He loves us, and that He will provide what we really need at the proper time. To help children learn contentment from the earliest age (even before they may seem to understand) work to give them a sense that God provides all that we really need. Once you personally realize how God provides, help children to come to a similar awareness with such statements as:

> Look what God has given us to use (or enjoy)!
>
> God just knew that we would need this right now.
>
> God knows that we aren't really ready yet to use or appreciate the . . . . we want.
>
> God probably has some things to teach us before giving us the . . . . we are asking Him for.
>
> God may want to give us something even better than the . . . . we have been asking Him for.
>
> Let's thank the Lord right now for giving us this (nice day, good trip, clothing, money for food, etc., etc., etc.,).

Before you can help your children become content in these ways, you must come to a real personal knowledge that God really does provide all that we have and need.

Contentment for ourselves and our children comes when we are able to look at all the things we already have for which to be thankful. We also need to know and then share with our children the wisdom (that we have perhaps learned the hard way) that things do not buy happiness.

The Lord Jesus demonstrated contentment even in awful situations. As He faced the cross, He prayed in the garden. He presented His desires to the Father but voiced a contentment with whatever the Father willed. The Bible says that He. . .

> . . .kneeled down, and prayed, Saying Father, if thou be willing, remove this cup from me: *nevertheless not my will, but thine, be done* (Luke 22:39-42).

NEATNESS AND ORDERLINESS

Although we live in a disorganized, confused world, God is not the author of this confusion. Everything He made is orderly. The stars stay in their proper places. The sun and the moon arrive exactly on schedule day by day and month by month through the year. The confused state of people's lives and the world is the result of sin. Confusion and disorder is rebellion against God for He commands:

> . . . let all things be done decently and in order (I Corinthians 14:40).

Neatness and orderliness have not been man's natural state since rebelling against God in the Garden. Therefore, these traits must be carefully trained and developed into the lives of our children. From their environment (the neatness of their rooms, and the organization of their schedules for eating, sleeping, being bathed, etc.) our children get very early concepts of either orderliness or disorganization. Parents must work at building orderliness into children's lives. In this way they learn to. . .

> . . .organize and care for their personal possessions.

> . . .give attention to personal grooming.

> . . .eat in a polite, orderly, mannerly way.

> . . .learn to write legibly.

Orderliness or neatness is defined as "preparing myself and my surroundings so that I can achieve the greatest efficiency." However, do not demand greater neatness than early finger dexterity and coordination make possible. But continually hold the goal of neatness before the child. For example, when the child first uses a spoon, and smears food all over his face trying to get it into his mouth, he should be encouraged and given the expectation that he will shortly learn to get all of the food into his mouth.

As the child gets a little older, concepts of neatness and order can be developed. As children help mother to sort socks by color or size into matching pairs, they learn principles of neatness and order. (This exercise will also develop visual discernment and concepts which will someday help the child learn to read.) Learning to stay within the lines in the coloring book (as finger dexterity permits) is another step.

As the child learns to dress and undress himself, he should be taught to place dirty clothes in the laundry hamper. When clothes are washed and dried, the child can be trained to place underwear, socks, and other clothing in the correct place in the bureau or in the closet.

Have places for children's toys. Train them to return all toys and personal possessions to the proper place when playtime is over, before meals or at bedtime. Training a child to do each of these tasks can take much longer than simply doing it for him. However, children who do not learn to be neat will suffer all of their lives.

The emphasis on neatness continues through the teen years. Additional requirements for making beds, cleaning their rooms, and maintaining the neatness of closets all must be added to what is expected as children grow and develop.

Neatness is important. The Lord Jesus placed a great emphasis on neatness and orderliness. This was illustrated when He fed the 5000 men plus women and children with five small rolls and two fishes. As He prepared to feed the great multitude, He told His disciples:

Make them sit down by fifties in a company (Luke 9:14).

After they were all seated in an orderly fashion, they were

fed. When all were full and finished, the Bible tells us:

> When they were filled, he said unto his disciples, *Gather up the fragments that remain, that nothing be lost* (John 6:12).

God commands, "Let all things be done decently and in order." Therefore, we must give our children a neat and orderly environment and train them to maintain it.

REVERENCE

Discipline problems in homes and schools today are widespread. Vandalism causes the senseless destruction of public and private property all across America. Never before have so many among young and old been destroying themselves emotionally, mentally and even physically. Cursing, gutter words for sex and parts of the body, and insults are heard everywhere. These are symptoms of a lack of reverence or respect in our society. Reverence was not deeply instilled into the character of children as they grew up. Reverence for authority, for those who are older, for the property of others, for God's Word, and for our flag are all vital to the health of our society. It is essential for order in the home, school, church, and community.

People who have no respect or reverence for those in authority will usually have very little regard for themselves and their peers either. Without self-respect and a sense of the importance of others, a person will fall into the abuse of his own body and person. He will not care for his appearance, dress, or speech. He will also manifest unkindness and discourtesy toward others. The lack of reverence and respect carries over into attitudes toward our country, its leaders, the flag, and the national anthem. Ultimately, the child who never learns to respect the things and people that God made will not have a proper respect or reverence toward God.

The lack of respect for others causes real problems for the teacher when the child starts to school. Lack of respect affects discipline. It also lies at the heart of many of the academic difficulties children experience. God explains why when He says:

> The fear [reverential trust] of the Lord *is the beginning of knowledge:* but fools despise wisdom and instruction (Proverbs 1:7).

According to the Bible, a person cannot hope to acquire true knowledge until he or she has an awe or reverence for the Lord. Respect for God will also produce respect for the authorities God uses to teach knowledge and wisdom.

To build reverent attitudes into children (and adults who missed this training when they were small), it is necessary to develop an awareness and recognition that. . .

. . .everyone we meet is a creature of God and therefore important. God gave each of us life. In addition, He also took the sins of every person and died for them so they can be saved and get a new life through His resurrected life.

In addition to the reverence everyone deserves, some should be given special respect. Parents, pastors, policemen, etc. are some of the people God has placed in special positions. They are responsible for teaching us, protecting us from danger, or supplying our needs. Others are important in other ways. God uses the handicapped and others with special needs to allow us to learn to give, and to develop patience, and love.

All property (our own and that of others) should be respected because God made it and it is owned by someone whom God made. When we take or destroy another person's property, we endanger his or her life or well-being to some extent. Because God gives us our property (clothes, toys, cars, homes, dishes, books), we should use them carefully.

By their attitudes, parents should start developing reverence in a baby as soon as he or she is born. Never holler or scream at a child. When a parent has lost his temper, a sincere apology as soon as possible shows respect for the child. The respect parents show for their own bodies, for each other, for their parents and in-laws, for the pastor, for policemen, for employers and for everyone will be *caught* by the child.

Teasing, cutting people down, and foolish jesting should never be done by the parents or tolerated in the children. TV cartoons do much to tear down reverence and respect for all that is good.

Children should never be given or allowed to wear clothes with slogans which build disrespect for themselves or others. That which encourages or glamorizes disrespectful behavior should also be banned. Parents must be vigilant

because the availability of "cute" stuff which builds disrespect is so widespread. For example, a leading national
chain offered a line of T-Shirts in its back-to-school specials
in 1981 which carried such slogans as. . .

"Kids Are Supposed to Goof Off"

"The Lab Called---Your Brain is Ready" (with an arrow
pointing to a pea-sized brain).

"Super Bad"

"Is That Your Nose---Or Are You Eating a Banana?"

Degrading shirts are also available for infants. They
have slogans such as:

"Grandma's Little Devil"

"My Parents Went to Florida and All I Got Was This Stupid
Shirt!"

Such slogans and shirts popularize and glamorize doing
wrong, cutting yourself or others down, etc.

Respect is built by avoiding that which is wrong and also
by training children in that which is right.

Boys learn respect for ladies when they see their fathers
stand when a woman enters the room, open the door for a
lady, or seat mother and daughters at the table. They
should be taught to do so as well.

Respect for God is developed as children see the time and
importance parents give to the Lord by reading and
studying His Word and obeying it. The attention and
reverence given to God's servants (missionaries, pastors,
and teachers) and our faithfulness in attending church
shows our own reverence for the Lord. How clean we keep
our bodies, how we dress, the care we give to the things God
gives us are other ways we show *and teach* reverence.

Every person needs to develop a reverent spirit. Reverence is a deep respect for God, for yourself, for others, and
for the property and possessions God gives to all of us. It is
sadly lacking in today's society.

FORGIVENESS

Troubles are mounting in America's homes, families,
churches and people. Troubles between people in the family,
church or at work get worse and worse because most people
do not see the necessity for forgiving. They do not know

how to forgive. Also, they will not genuinely seek forgiveness when they have wronged others.

Consider how unforgiving attitudes are behind most of these tragic statistics:

. . .nearly one out of two marriages end in divorce.

. . .2.5-million young people ran away from home in recent years, many never to be heard from again.

. . .over 80% of all Christian young people do not have a really meaningful relationship with their parents.

. . .almost all young people and many adults regularly try to blot out the real world and its hurts with rock music.

. . .child abuse, wife beating, husband battering and granny bashing are all approaching epidemic levels.

These and many other symptoms of sickness in our society stem directly from wrongs and hurts which have not been forgiven.

Teaching a child how to forgive and how to be forgiven from an early age can protect him or her from being a behavior problem in school. Knowing how to stay right with others as a result of forgiving and being forgiven can keep your child from becoming a bitter vandal or one who seeks escape in dope or alcohol. It can keep a child from looking to materialism to escape from real life. Unless children can forgive and be forgiven and maintain good family relationships thereby, they often seek to establish deep emotional relationships outside the family too early. The inability to forgive leads to broken marriages later in life.

Learning to forgive can protect us from Satanic harassment and torment in our lives. The Apostle Paul warned the church at Corinth to forgive a man who had repented of awful sin. . .

. . . lest Satan should get an advantage of us, for we are not ignorant of his devices (II Corinthians 2:11).

The Lord Jesus set the standard for forgiveness. He told Peter that he had to forgive seventy times seven times. He warned that a person who has received forgiveness from God will be turned over to the tormentors by the Heavenly Father if. . .

. . .ye from your hearts forgive not everyone his brother their trespasses (Matthew 18:35).

We are commanded to forgive. In Ephesians 4:32 the Apostle Paul encouraged believers this way:

> And be ye kind one to another, tenderhearted, forgiving one another, even as God for Christ's sake hath forgiven you.

To teach forgiveness, you must recognize the importance of being a forgiving person yourself. To learn how to forgive, see how God forgives us. Then develop the same attitudes toward those who have offended and wronged us. God's forgiveness has seven wonderful characteristics. They are:

1. Forgiveness can be granted only after the punishment for sin has been satisfied. The Bible teaches that ". . .without the shedding of blood there is no remission [forgiveness]" (Hebrews 9:22). Even though sin requires the shedding of blood and death, God so wanted us to be free to come to Him and be reconciled that He took all the shame, guilt, blame, and punishment upon Himself. He made our sins His own. He paid the full price for our sins when He died on the cross. Seeing His willingness to make our sins His own brings us to confess our wrongdoing and to seek forgiveness.

We should have the same willingness to take the blame on ourselves in seeking to have right relationships restored between ourselves and others.

2. Once sin is forgiven, it should never be brought up again---even if the offense is repeated. This is how God forgives us. He promises that once He forgives sinners that. . .

> . . .their sins and iniquities will I remember no more (Hebrews 10:17).

3. Forgiveness comes as a result of confession. Confession is agreeing, without any excuses or conditions, with God's judgment of our actions. When we seek forgiveness from someone else, we should confess our wrongs clearly and plainly and without excuses. God promises:

> If we confess our sins, he is faithful and just to forgive us our sins and to cleanse us from all unrighteousness (I John 1:9).

4. Forgiveness is the basis for restored fellowship. God says:

I have blotted out, as a thick cloud, thy transgressions, and as a cloud, thy sins: *return unto me;* for I have redeemed thee (Isaiah 44:22).

5. Forgiveness produces a response of love in us for God. It should also cause those who have been forgiven to love, once they have been forgiven by others. The Lord Jesus taught:

Wherefore I say unto thee, Her sins, which are many, are forgiven; for she loved much: but to whom little is forgiven, the same loveth little (Luke 7:47).

6. Being forgiven is a reason for rejoicing. We are taught this by the Lord Jesus Himself. The Scripture says:

And, behold, they brought to him a man sick of the palsy, lying on a bed: and Jesus seeing their faith said unto the sick of the palsy; *Son, be of good cheer; thy sins be forgiven thee.* (Matthew 9:2).

7. Forgiveness is the basis for blessedness in life. Blessedness is a state of happiness, completeness, fulfillment, and satisfaction. In Psalm 32, the Bible says:

Blessed is he whose transgression is forgiven, whose sin is covered. Blessed is the man unto whom the Lord imputeth not iniquity, and in whose spirit there is no guile.

When I kept silence, my bones waxed old through my roaring all the day long. For day and night thy hand was heavy upon me: my moisture is turned into the drought of summer. Selah.

I acknowledged my sin unto thee, and mine iniquity I have not hid. I said, I will confess my transgressions unto the Lord; and thou forgavest the iniquity of my sins. Selah.

How do we teach our children to forgive? By our example and our willingness to forgive. And by our own seeking of forgiveness when it is needed. Be quick to acknowledge and confess any way in which you have wronged your child. Seek forgiveness and explain what results. Also be quick to forgive the child once wrongs have been righted and punishments have been fulfilled.

Be alert to discern when children are "hurting" over something. Get to the bottom of the problem. Do whatever is necessary to enable them to forgive. Do not just count on their "getting over it." The things we "get over" but never really forgive are like festering sores which have healed on the surface. While they may look to be healed they will break out again under pressure.

The Lord Jesus is our model. When He hung on the cross, He had been placed there by wicked, unbelieving, cruel, mocking men. Even so He looked to His Father and cried out:

> Father, forgive them; for they know not what they do. (Luke 23:34).

GRATEFULNESS

Developing an attitude of gratefulness and a thankful spirit in a child's character will help him have a contented, happy life. Being grateful will also protect children from becoming homosexuals and from having lives filled with violence and crime. As amazing as it may seem, God says that because men were not thankful for how He made them that. . .

> . . .for this cause God gave them up unto vile affections; for even their women did change the natural use into that which is against nature: And likewise also the men, leaving the natural use of the woman, burned in their lust one toward another; men with men working that which is unseemly (Romans 1:26-27).

Once individuals move from being unthankful into these perversions, the Scripture says that God gives them over. . .

> . . .to a reprobate mind, to do those things which are not convenient.... fornication, wickedness, covetousness, maliciousness; full of envy, murder, debate, deceit, malignity, whisperers, backbiters, haters of God, despiteful, proud, boasters, inventors of evil things, disobedient to parents, without understanding, covenant breakers, without natural affection, implacable, unmerciful. . . (Romans 1:28-31).

These verses record the whole path downward into homosexuality, perversion and sin. It starts when a person who knows that God exists and that He made the world and all that is in it, refuses to glorify God for all that He is. This starts the individual down an awful path. The Scripture says:

> Because that when they knew God they glorified him not as God, *neither were thankful;* but became vain in their imaginations, and their foolish heart was darkened. Professing themselves to be wise, they became fools (Romans 1:21-22).

The child who never develops a grateful spirit will travel an awful road. On the plus side, however, being thankful brings joy and peace---even in difficult times and situations. The Bible says:

> Rejoice in the Lord alway: and again I say, Rejoice...Be careful [anxious] for nothing; but in every thing by prayer and supplication *with thanksgiving* let your requests be made known unto God, And the peace of God which passeth all understanding, shall keep your hearts and minds through Christ Jesus (Philippians 4:4, 6-7).

That is why in I Thessalonians 5:18 God commands....

> In every thing give thanks: for this is the will of God in Christ Jesus concerning you.

So, we are to be thankful in everything. Thankful attitudes and actions must grow out of faith that...

> God is all powerful, in control of everything, all wise, all knowing and all good and all loving.

Even though all of these things about God are true, very few people are truly thankful or express their thanks. For example, when the Lord Jesus healed ten lepers of their awful disease, only one returned to thank him (see Luke 17:11-18).

How can the trait of gratefulness be developed in our children? There are many steps including:

> ...giving God credit and thanks for everything. Build understanding with your words and the Words of the Bible that God is in control, that He is all powerful, all wise, all knowing and all good and loving. Explain that because God has these attributes, He will bring good out of even those things which appear to be bad. (Read Romans 8:28-29)

Children should be trained to say "thank you" as soon as they start to talk. Thanks should be given for food, for anything which is given to them or done for them. What the mouth is trained to confess (thanks) will become real in the heart. Develop thanksgiving in all forms. If a gift arrives from Grandma or Grandpa for Christmas or a birthday, teach the child to say "thank you." Sit down with the child even at a very young age and write "thank-you" notes for them.

Help children to develop thankfulness to God for making them boys or girls. Be careful not to glorify or glamorize the opposite sex. A parent who casually says, "If you were a girl (or a boy) we could do thus and so together," can do real harm to a child. In the same way, care should be taken to dress boys as boys and girls as girls and encourage each to develop their masculinity or femininity to the fullest. A child also needs to learn to be thankful that God made him just right for the life He has for him.

Mothers and fathers should be careful to build up their partners to the children (even when a divorce or separation may have destroyed the home). By the same token each parent should be all he or she should be. The little boy who has a no-good father can grow up bitter. He will fear growing up to be a man like his father. Children should be thankful for both parents and for whatever sex God made them.

Children born with handicaps and those who acquire them later through accidents need to learn to be thankful. The Scripture in John 9:1-41 can be helpful. Jesus' disciples, seeing a man born blind, asked the Lord, "Who did sin, this man or his parents, that he was born blind?" Jesus explained that neither case was true. The man was born blind so "that the works of God should be made manifest in him." Then the Lord healed him.

Not everyone gets healed, but handicaps can bring glory to God. Fanny Crosby was blind for most of her ninety-five years. Although blind physically, she developed spiritual vision which has been rivaled by few down through history. God used her to write more of the songs in widely-used hymn books than any other person.

A little two year old girl named Betty Rice lost her hearing. Her folks developed ways to teach her the Bible. What they learned grew into a ranch in Tennessee where thousands of deaf people have heard the Gospel and been saved. Others have been trained at the Bill Rice Ranch to start ministries for deaf people in hundreds of Bible-believing churches. Betty Rice's deafness has been greatly used of God.

God knows best about everything. He promises to bring good out of all things for those who love Him. Therefore, we can thank Him in faith for every experience in life. As we learn to be thankful and demonstrate our gratefulness, we can teach children to be thankful as well.

The Lord Jesus was an example for us. He regularly exhibited a grateful spirit. In John 6:1-14 when He fed the 5000, He gave thanks. The Scripture says:

> And Jesus took the loaves; and when he had given thanks, he distributed to the disciples, and the disciples to them that were set down; and likewise of the fishes as much as they would. (John 6:11)

He is our model. We, too, are to be thankful in everything.

FAITH

Everyone needs faith. Nearly all of us exercise faith in *something* at *some time* in life. When we accept a check in payment for work, we do it in faith that it is "good." We believe that we can exchange it for real money. Even when we are paid paper money or coins for labor or goods, we must receive them in faith that they can later be exchanged for food, gasoline, clothes, or something else we need or want.

Those who believe that God made the world are sometimes ridiculed. They are laughed at for basing their belief on "faith rather than facts." However, there are no facts to support evolution. The idea that all life evolved from green slime through a series of accumulated accidents requires faith. Is it more logical to believe that an entire orderly universe came about through a series of accidents—or that there is an all-powerful, all-knowing, all-wise, all-good God who made it all just as He says in His Word that He did?

Everyone has faith in something. Children need to be trained to have faith in those whose word can be trusted. They should have faith in their parents, the pastor, their teachers, and others who show they can be trusted to do what they say. They need to be given faith in an all-good, all-knowing, all powerful, all-loving God.

Faith, in its simplest form, is just trusting someone to do what he has promised and acting upon it. The degree of faith which can be exercised in a person depends on actually hearing what was said or promised, determining whether or not he or she really means what was said, and then deciding whether or not the person making the commitment actually has the power and ability to do what is promised.

How do we instill faith in our children? First, we must always keep our word. We must be careful to *do* what we promise. It must be done *on time*. Commitments should be fulfilled *exactly*. We must deliver promised stories, playtime, treats, gifts, rewards, trips, etc. Fulfilling promised discipline is just as important as giving promised rewards or treats.

Whenever we fail, we must be quick to acknowledge fully our wrongdoing or failure to the child and seek forgiveness. Such occasions are an opportunity to point out to your child that as humans we can fail but that God never fails.

Exercise extreme care to be very specific and definite about promises. A vague remark such as "Someday I might build you a treehouse" or "Maybe we can go to Grandma's next week if everything works out" is an ironclad "promise" to a small child. Training children to listen—to be attentive, to really know what you say—is important. Help them to understand by being specific and definite in what you say and promise. *Then keep your word.*

To avoid faith-destroying experiences children should be under the influence and authority only of those whose words can be trusted and believed. Babysitters, pastors, teachers, and friends, must be chosen with care. Otherwise, children can develop an unhealthy, cynical attitude toward everyone. This will ultimately hinder them from believing and trusting the Lord for salvation and the needs of life.

Faith in God involves visualizing what God will do in any situation and then acting in accordance with what God promises. We learn from the Bible what God promises. The most important single factor in developing a child's faith in God is to live a life of faith yourself—and let the child know and see it. Learn how to trust God rather than the finance company for the needs of your family. God will show you how to save and manage. He will also do some real miracles for those who are wholeheartedly trusting Him and praying. Use these occasions to teach your children. Pray together about needs—and then rejoice when God provides.

God promises blessings and success to those who read

His Word daily and meditate in it. God says that faith comes from hearing His Word (Romans 10:17). That makes sense. We cannot have real faith unless we know what God promises to do. Look for God's promises as you read the Bible.

As we mature in our ability to take God at His Word for health, finances, food, shelter, obedience, and everything, our children will grow up learning to "live by faith" also.

TRUTHFULNESS

Each character trait is essential for a happy, well-adjusted, stable, productive, fruitful life. Each character trait is essential if we are to be pleasant company, to have friends, and to work well with, for, and over others. As essential as each character trait is, one seems even more essential than others. That is truthfulness.

Truthfulness must start with "me." Unless a person can be completely honest with himself, he will never be able to accept himself as he is. Without truthfulness he will never be able to seek help in strengthening weak areas because he will not be able to be honest about his needs.

Being completely honest with ourselves is the most difficult step. It must be followed by determining to be totally and completely honest with God and others. Without truthfulness, a person will live a life of excusing himself, covering up, and exaggeration. He will be isolated from others by the wall of falsehoods and distortions which he erects to hide behind. He will live with the constant fear of exposure of lies told to avoid the consequences of mistakes and failures.

Without being truthful, a person will never be able to seek and enjoy the forgiveness and cleansing from God and others which is dependent on truthfully acknowledging the need to be forgiven. Without truthfulness a person is doomed to having his word questioned and scrutinized or just ignored *even when he is telling the truth*.

To escape the tragedy of living a life of deception in later life, a child must learn to be truthful from infancy on. *Truthfulness is a way of earning future trust by accurately reporting past facts and events*. Being truthful involves learning to be a reliable messenger, carefully reporting facts and attitudes. A child needs to learn to gain the approval of others without misrepresenting facts. If a child is to be truthful, he or she must face the consequences of a mistake---or even deliberate disobedience.

The Bible should be used in developing the desire for truthfulness. God says that one of the duties of a Christian is. . .

> . . .putting away lying (Ephesians 4:25).

The Bible probably speaks more harshly about the sin of lying and deceit than any other single offense against God. Proverbs 12:22 sums up God's attitude towards lying this way:

> Lying lips are an abomination to the Lord: but they that deal truly are his delight.

In Revelation 21:7-8 God includes liars among the "real bad" sinners who will burn in hell forever. Consider these verses:

> He that overcometh shall inherit all things; and I will be his God, and he shall be my son. But the fearful, and unbelieving, and the abominable, and murderers, and whoremongers, and sorcerers, and idolaters, and *all liars*, shall have their part in the lake which burneth with fire and brimstone; which is the second death.

God confirms the doom of liars a few verses later in Revelation 21:27. After describing the beauties and glories of heaven, He says:

> And there shall in no wise enter into it anything that defileth, neither whatsoever worketh abomination, *or maketh a lie:* but they which are written in the Lamb's book of life (Revelation 21:27).

So, truthfulness is important for this life---and for eternity. How do we develop truthfulness in a child? There are about half a dozen basic guidelines to follow. They include:

1. Make your own life an example of truthfulness. Tell the truth even when ducking a salesman at the door or on the telephone or in explaining why you missed church on Sunday. Always tell your children the truth. Many Christian parents do not fool their children into believing that Santa Claus is real. The truth must ultimately come out. Children sometimes become disillusioned when it does. The

child who finds out Santa Claus is not real can later wonder if someday he will find out that God is a myth also.

2. Make the punishment for lying far exceed any momentary benefit or satisfaction gained by it. John Wesley's mother said that cowardice and fear of punishment often lead children into lying until they get the custom of it which they can not leave. To prevent this, a law was made that whoever was charged with a fault of which they were guilty would not be beaten if they would completely confess it and promise to amend. This rule prevented a good deal of lying."

3. Reduce punishment for offenses when the child tells the truth immediately and completely when asked, if he has not actually been caught "red-handed."

4. Be truthful and open about your own shortcomings and failures in dealing with your children and others. Seek forgiveness when you have created a wrong impression by not being completely honest.

5. Start *early* to teach the child Scriptures about truthfulness and the evils of lying.

6. Praise truthfulness. Share stories like the one about how George Washington admitted it when he cut down the cherry tree and about Abraham Lincoln's honesty as a boy.

Never accuse a child of lying unless you have absolute proof. Do not make an accusation based only on circumstantial evidence. When you suspect a child has lied, prayerfully ask God either to convict the child and bring him to repentance or expose the lie. A real aid in building truthfulness is for the child to come to realize that Numbers 32:23 is really true. This Scripture says:

. . .be sure your sin will find your out.

SECURITY

Each of us needs to be secure. Children not only need to *be* secure and safe but also need a *sense* of security. To avoid fears, to achieve in school, to maintain a good digestive system, to sleep restfully, etc., etc., etc. children and adults need to feel secure.

The needed sense of security must ultimately stem from the knowledge that God is all powerful, all knowing, all caring, all loving *and* all wise. Because God is all of these things, we can be secure in the faith that He will take care of us even when circumstances do not seem to be showing it.

The sense of security which everyone needs to be truly happy is really the product of faith in God.

Hopes for the future must be built on the Lord and His promises rather than material possessions, our abilities, job security, government programs, and pension plans, *all of which can be taken away.* God never changes. In the Old Testament, Job lost his possessions, his family, his friends, and his health. Even so, he was secure because he could say in faith . . .

> Though He slay me, yet will I trust him: but I will maintain mine own ways before him. He also shall be my salvation . . . . For I know that my redeemer liveth, and that He shall stand at the latter day upon the earth: And though after my skin worms destroy this body, yet in my flesh shall I see God (Job 13:15-16a; 19:25-26).

Naturally, a child is not born with this kind of faith and sense of security. A baby lives in the mother's womb with total security (if the mother is secure and her emotions and physical state are not in turmoil). The baby, through struggle, comes out of the womb into a world where there are many causes for anxiety. Parents have the duty and responsibility to build an environment where the child will develop a sense of security.

Security will develop and deepen as parents can be depended upon to provide warmth and to feed and bathe on schedule. As the child is surrounded by love, he can be secure even at times when normal schedules and activities are disrupted.

Elizabeth Handford grew up in a family of six girls. She was the daughter of the well-known and well-loved evangelist, Dr. John R. Rice. She is the wife of Dr. Walter Handford, pastor of Southside Baptist Church in Greenville, S.C. She is a mother and has helped many other wives and mothers to fulfill their God-given roles. In emphasizing the importance of building security into lives of children, she says that to rear good children who are happy . . . .

> . . . the first thing is to raise them in a home that is absolutely stable in a world of change. This is a home where the husband and wife love each other and say so and express it. They provide a home which is a Rock of Gibraltar for the children. The home and parents must be unchangeable no matter how

other things may change.

This security will develop, Mrs. Handford says, when children know . . .

> . . . that there is a profound, deep love for them that has nothing to do with their worthiness or unworthiness. In fact, the more rebellious they are the more they need to know that you really love them.

In an age when half of all marriages are ending in divorce, children are exposed at a very young age to other children whose homes have been destroyed by divorce. To maintain their sense of security, they need to know that their own homes are secure. Mrs. Handford encourages parents to build this needed security. She says:

> Kids ought to see the right kind of relationship between the husband and wife. This is so important. It builds security—and it is where they will learn to do it themselves.

As the children grow, parents should work to transfer the basis for the child's security gradually from themselves to the Lord. However, the child who grows up in an insecure environment without the security which comes from good earthly parents, will have difficulty in finding security in the Heavenly Father.

MEEKNESS

People who demand their own way and are constantly guarding their own rights are miserable to live with. They are also usually miserable themselves. They are always ready to do battle. They are usually angry inside. They feel "done to" even if they get their own way 90% of the time.

A meek person is one who has learned how to yield personal rights and possessions to God. Once all rights and possessions are surrendered to God, He can be trusted to provide needs. He can be trusted to "even the score" if it needs evening. The Lord can be trusted to care for and protect the possessions we have given Him which He allows us to use. A meek person has learned how to handle anger which arises when personal rights to property, courtesy and fairness are violated. A meek person earns the right to be heard rather than to demand a hearing.

At the same time, a meek person is not a namby-pamby doormat nor an easy target for every would-be con man.

Moses, for example, was the leader over 3-million of God's people for forty years. He was certainly the greatest man in the Old Testament. The Scripture tells us that with all of his qualities of leadership Moses was . . .

> . . .very meek, above all the men which were upon the face of the earth (Numbers 12:3).

Moses always stook up for God's glory and honor. Yet, he never demanded his own personal rights. A meek person is someone who never does anything on his own. He seeks and waits for God's direction in everything. Once the meek person knows what God wants, he can be very bold in following the Lord and His instructions.

The Lord Jesus is the supreme and superb example of meekness. He said of His relationship to His Father. . . .

> . . .I do always those things that please Him. (John 8:29a)

For this reason, He could say . . .

> . . .Come unto me, all ye that labour and are heavy laden, and I will give you rest. Take my yoke upon you, and learn of me; *for I am meek and lowly in heart:* and ye shall find rest unto your souls. For my yoke is easy and my burden is light (Matthew 11:28-30).

He gives us rest because He carries our burdens rather than making us do our part. When He, God, came to earth and became a man, He gave us the perfect example of meekness. He yielded His rights to be bowed down to so that He could serve and benefit others. Philippians 2:5-8 says:

> Let this mind be in you, which was also in Christ Jesus: who being in the form of God, thought it not robbery to be equal with God: But made himself of no reputation, and took upon him the form of a servant, and was made in the likeness of men: And being found in fashion as a man, he humbled himself, and became obedient unto death, even the death of the cross.

He who was God became a servant. Rather than guarding His own state of sinlessness, He took our sin with its guilt and shame and made it His own. He was not forced to go to the cross. He told the soldiers who came to take Him:

> . . . Thinkest thou that I cannot now pray to my Father, and he shall presently give me more than twelve legions of angels? But

how then shall the scriptures be fulfilled that thus it must be? (Matthew 26:53-54).

He was meek and lowly and gave Himself for us. We are called to be and do the same. Such a life of yielding rights and expectations is not a life of misery but a life of happiness, joy, peace, and complete fulfillment and satisfaction, for the Scripture says:

Blessed are the meek: for they shall inherit the earth (Matthew 5:5).

It is vitally important to be meek. To accept both the guidance and teaching we need from God and others, we must be meek. (See Psalm 25:9). Only a meek person really hears the Gospel through which he can be saved. The Lord Jesus said:

The Spirit of the Lord God is upon me; because the Lord hath anointed me to preach good tidings [the gospel] *to the meek* (Isaiah 61:1).

We are not meek by nature. We all want our own way. We all desire to do "our own thing." We all seek and demand recognition. We selfishly hold on to our own possessions even when we don't really need them. Such manifestations of self-will in our children need to be dealt with calmly and lovingly if a child is to be taught meekness.

Truly, meekness probably cannot be "taught"—it must be "caught." As we rear our children, we must demonstrate an even-tempered meekness. Whenever we get angry, we must acknowledge our failure and ask children for forgiveness. We must teach our children to be respectful rather than to demand respect from them. We must be careful not to get upset if we do not get prompt attention and service in a store or restaurant.

We can and should work to develop the character trait of meekness in ourselves and our children. However, true meekness and the blessedness which comes with it is the result of being filled with God's Spirit. Working to develop meekness as a character trait will prepare the person to experience meekness as a fruit of God's Spirit on a regular and consistent basis.

CAUTIOUSNESS

We live in a rash age. The slogan for many is, "If it feels good, do it." A big percentage of the current generation has gotten mixed up in premarital sex, drugs, the occult, protests, marriage, heavy financial commitments, and deep debt. Very few have given much thought to the long-range consequences.

Without a sense of cautiousness, an individual can rush into a bad or dangerous situation without thinking. Being cautious can also protect us from messing up something which is basically good by doing it at the wrong time or in the wrong way.

The Bible warns of the dangers of acting without thinking a situation through. Proverbs 19:2 says:

> . . . . and he that hasteth with his feet sinneth.

Cautiousness is the quality of carefully evaluating the possible consequences of decisions and actions before acting. Cautiousness involves . . .

> . . . learning that unfamiliar situations may contain danger.
>
> . . . gaining adequate advice and counsel before making decisions.
>
> . . . seeing future consequences of actions and decisions made now.
>
> . . . knowing the importance of right timing in carrying out right decisions.
>
> . . . learning how to detect and avoid evil and ungodly people and recognizing temptations and fleeing them.

A child must be trained to be cautious. However, wisdom is needed to train children to be cautious without giving them unnecessary fears.

Developing cautiousness in a child starts with warnings concerning dangers in the house. A child becomes more cautious by ignoring warnings and experiencing the pain caused by a stove burn or from water that is too hot. Eating food which has not cooled sufficiently adds to the lesson. Uncomfortable lessons learned in these areas can prevent tragedies in more serious situations. Learning cautiousness early in the home will cause the child to accept and heed warnings and even develop his own sense of cautiousness about . . .

> . . . dangers in crossing streets.
>
> . . . the opposite sex (and perverts of the same sex).
>
> . . . playing in water.
>
> . . . drinking unknown substances.

As young people grow up, they will encounter all sorts of temptations. The most dangerous are the "sugar-coated" ones. These are those which are accompanied by challenges from the crowd such as . . .

> ". . . how can you know if you don't try it?"
>
> ". . . a little bit never hurt anyone."
>
> ". . . we'll be careful to stop in time."
>
> ". . . don't be a 'fraidy cat."
>
> ". . . no one will ever know."

Such arguments should be warning flags to the child or young person schooled to be cautious.

A realization must be developed in children that God makes parents responsible for their protection. Physical dangers are usually obvious. However, as children grow they should be aware of the caution exercised by parents in watching TV, the types of music listened to, etc. Guidelines can be established. For example, some families make it a rule that whenever a TV series uses a curse word, that program or series is scratched off the "acceptable" list. Similar guides are established for programs which show adultery and certain types of violence, or which are irreverent and laugh at God. Parents can explain to children that listening to TV characters cuss will open the door to using such language ourselves at some future time of stress or disappointment. Cautions concerning TV and cursing instilled in children will carry over. Children so taught will tend to be cautious as they get older about friends who use bad language, for example.

Parents have this responsibility to explain to children the hidden and/or disguised dangers in our environment. Children should be shown, for example, how watching "fun" cartoons where characters are "lippy" and disrespectful or are constantly "bopping" one another can make us tolerant of such behavior. We will eventually end up doing the behavior we first tolerate or laugh at. This danger is very real all through life. For the wife who has "lived through" many divorces in daytime TV soap operas divorce becomes an acceptable and even logical solution for marriage difficulties.

In building cautiousness into a child, parents should share the lessons they have learned the hard way. Hopefully, as the child learns from the parent, he or she will not also have to learn by experiencing pain.

There are many things to be cautious about. On shopping trips, children can be shown that boxes and containers sometimes have deceptive shapes which make them look bigger.

Point out that advertisements which show glamourous-looking people drinking in glamourous places never picture cars demolished by drunken drivers and the mangled bodies of their victims. They do not show little children beaten by a drunken father or the unpaid bills which pile up because father drinks up the family's income. While cigarette packages and advertising must warn of dangers to health from smoking, beer ads do not have to warn that one of every nine people who have the first drink becomes a problem drinker.

Developing the character trait of cautiousness will help children avoid many pitfalls and tragedies through life.

PATIENCE

Would you like to develop a character trait into your children which will protect them from getting in trouble sexually and having to get married someday?

Would you like to help your children avoid life-long financial difficulties and keep them from living all of their lives in the bondage caused by debt?

Would you like to protect your child from being involved in an automobile accident later in life?

Would you like to help your child grow up to enjoy life---to have peace and freedom from turmoil---to avoid ulcers and high blood pressure?

There is one character trait which is the key to achieving these desirable goals. Patience is essential for real happiness and success in life.

Patience is learning how to wait contentedly to fulfill personal desires, wants and goals. Having patience increases the time you can wait between achievement and reward. Learning how to accept difficult situations as being from God without giving Him a deadline to remove them is a key to developing patience.

Developing patience as a child will help avoid sexual temptations as a teen-ager or young adult. The patient person will wait until the proper time to fulfill his desires and wants.

Impatiently wanting something "right now" leads many people to buy things on credit which they cannot really afford. Instead of patiently waiting and saving the money, purchases are made on credit. Because of high interest charges, high premiums are paid for what is bought. Frequently, things are worn out before they are paid for.

The person who is patient can avoid speeding violations, running stop signs, and passing on a curve or too near the top of a hill. Each of these increase the risk of auto accidents and serious injury or death.

Training children to be patient will protect them from much grief later in life. It will also make them a lot more pleasant to be around as they grow up and when they become adults. Some helps in building patience include:

> Establish a schedule for a baby's feeding and stick to it. The "demand" feeding fad of letting children eat whenever they seem to be demanding it builds bad habits. (Of course, if a child is consistently hungry for a considerable period before scheduled feedings, the amount or types of food needs to be increased).

> When children stumble and fall when learning to walk or fail when developing some other new skill, do not rush to help or pick them up. Doing so will hinder them from developing the patience to persevere until they succeed.

> Children should not be permitted to snack between meals.

> Never permit children to get birthday or Christmas gifts in advance of the actual day.

> Do not stimulate the desires of children to be older than they are. Putting children in clothes which are too old for them, learning to drive before they are of legal age, buying motorbikes for children who should be just getting a bicycle, and dating too

early all foster the impatient streak which each of us has.

God has a proper time for all things in our lives. We need to learn, recognize, and wait for God's timing. We need to teach our children to do the same. God tells us this in Ecclesiastes 3:1-8.

> To every thing there is a season, and a time to every purpose under heaven.
>
> A time to be born, and a time to die; a time to plant and a time to pluck up that which is planted; a time to kill, and a time to heal; a time to break down, and a time to build up;
>
> A time to weep, and a time to laugh; a time to mourn, and a time to dance; a time to cast away stones, and a time to gather stones together; a time to embrace, and a time to refrain from embracing.
>
> A time to get and a time to lose; a time to keep, and a time to cast away; a time to rend, and a time to sew; a time to keep silence, and a time to speak; a time to love, and a time to hate; a time of war and a time of peace.

The key to happiness is learning the proper time for all things---and waiting patiently for that time.

SUMMARY

Parents who dedicate themselves to instilling needed character traits into their children will not stop with these. They also will not stop the process when the child starts school. Once character building is a part of family life, other essential traits can be added as children grow. Among them are determination, diligence, punctuality, thriftiness, dependability, flexibility, generosity and loyalty.

Chapter IX

YOUR CHILDREN WILL BE WHAT YOU ARE

> *And Adam lived an hundred and thirty years, and begat a son in his own likeness, after his image; and called his name Seth.*
>
> *--Genesis 5:3*

CHILDREN are not likely to be better adjusted, happier, or more successful in life than their parents are. This premise is Biblical. Adam and Eve, for example, raised a son, Seth. The Bible says that Seth grew up in Adam's "own likeness, after his image."

Proverbs 22:6 tells why. It says: "Train up a child in the way he should go and when he is old, he will not depart from it." Parents cannot successfully train their children to be more than they are themselves. Children learn to walk, talk, and eat by example. Their personalities, attitudes, reactions, and desires largely mirror those of their parents. *Your child will be what you are.*

Much research supports this premise. Statistics show, for example, that divorce runs in families. If parents are divorced the likelihood is that the marriages of their children will fail also. Those who get pregnant before marriage, have a baby out of wedlock, or have an abortion are more likely to see their children experience the same tragedies.

Logic indicates that if children see or experience difficult or tragic circumstances in their families, they will work hard to avoid repeating these problems in their own lives. It does not work that way in practice, however. Consider these facts:

Studies of case histories indicate that children of alcoholics are much more likely to become alcoholics themselves.

Statistics in the field of child abuse show the same pattern:

> ...people, who were themselves abused, sexually molested, etc. as children are much more likely to abuse their own children.

Children become what their parents are. Behavior patterns repeat in generation after generation. Those who have problems with bitterness, unforgiveness, immorality, lying, or rebellion against parents will see the same patterns repeated in their own children. It happens in spite of all safeguards parents may try to erect to protect children from repeating their mistakes, failures and sin. It happens in spite of children's determination not to be like their parents. It happens in spite of the determination of young parents not to subject their own children to the hurts they have experienced. More than just bad example is involved. The tragedies repeat even though the parents' sin took place long before the child was born. The pattern of sin and failure is repeated even when a child has been adopted at an early age and never knew his or her natural parents.

The Bible tells why. In the Ten Commandments, God says:

> I am the Lord thy God, which have brought thee out of the land of Egypt, out of the house of bondage. Thou shalt have no other gods before me. Thou shalt not make unto thee any graven image, or any likeness of anything that is in heaven above, or that is in the earth beneath, or that is in the water under the earth.
> Thou shalt not bow down thyself to them, nor serve them; for *I the Lord thy God am a jealous God, visiting the iniquity of the fathers upon the children unto the third and fourth generation of them that hate me;* And shewing mercy unto thousands of them that love me, and keep my commandments (Exodus 20:2-6).

God says here that those who worship, obey, and serve false gods will see their children do the same thing. False gods are more than idols or statues. A god can be anything which controls a person. A false god can be anything looked to for approval, pleasure, satisfaction, protection, or fulfillment of needs. Those who let themselves be controlled by such a false god will see their children follow the same path.

That the danger is real is illustrated many times in the Bible. As mentioned, it can happen even though the specific sin occurred long before the child was born. In Genesis 12:10-20, for example, Abraham quit trusting God during a famine. He sought food in Egypt for himself and his wife. Because he did not trust God to provide in the land God had given him, when he arrived in Egypt he was not able to trust the Lord to protect himself and his wife. He became fearful that the Egyptians would kill him to get his beautiful wife, Sarai. To protect himself, he denied that Sarai was his wife. He arranged for her to go into Pharaoh's harem.

In spite of Abraham's lack of faith, God protected Sarai in the situation. Although Abraham lost face in the sight of the Egyptians, it all seemed to work out finally for good. However, twenty-five years later Abraham and Sarai had a son. His name was Isaac. When Isaac was himself forty years old another famine came to the land. Isaac then repeated all his father's sins. He failed to stay in the land and trust the Lord for food. When he went to Gerar seeking food, he feared that men would kill him for his wife. He also denied that Rebekah was his wife. Like his father, he put his wife in the harem of a foreign king. The sad story did not stop there either. Almost 200 years after Abraham's original sin of failing to trust God for food in a famine, his grandson did the same thing. Jacob took his entire family to Egypt seeking food in a time of famine. As a result, the children of Israel spent hundreds of years in slavery in Egypt. It all started with Abraham's sin of not trusting God. God records the continuing story of the "sins of the fathers" in Genesis 12:10-20, 26:1-16 and 41:54-50:26 and Exodus 1:1-14.

Truly the sins of the fathers (and mothers) do show up in children *for generations.** How you live, therefore is important. Not only will you suffer the consequences of wrong standards, values, and attitudes, but your children, your

----

*Upon seeing this truth, you may realize that some of your own personal struggles are the result of the "sins of the fathers." Do not despair. God has provided a way of deliverance from the bondage of hereditary sins. His Word says that the "sins of the fathers" are upon the children---not

grandchildren and your great-grandchildren may also. *Your children will be what you are.*

To give children a right start in life, parents need to build happy, successful Christian lives for themselves. Then they can train their children to follow in their footsteps.

Do you want your children to be loving—to have lives of peace and joy? Do you want children who are good—children who are gentle and do not demand their "rights?" Do you want children who are kind, faithful, and self-controlled? Do you want a child who will be loved by neighbors, teachers, and others? Do you want your child to grow up to love, honor and obey God and be sure of going to heaven when this life ends? These are some of the characteristics and blessings of a happy, successful Christian life. They can only be enjoyed consistently by God-centered, Spirit-filled Christians.

If children are to enjoy happy successful Christian lives, their parents need to have Spirit-filled lives. A God-centered, Spirit-filled Christian life is a life through which God is free to continually show His presence, His power, and His love continually. God will manifest His presence and power in and through the life of any person who follows God's blueprint for life as set forth in the Bible, His Word.

There are seven prerequisites for a God-centered, Spirit-

----

just the penalty or effects of them. Therefore the sin of your fathers is actually on you. Even though it may not have caused you difficulty yet, it can in the future. Confession is the only way to be cleansed from sin. In I John 1:8-9, the Bible says: "If we say we have no sin, we deceive ourselves and the truth is not in us. If we confess our sins, he is faithful and just to forgive us our sins and to cleanse us from all unrighteousness." Leviticus 26:40-42 tells us that confession is also the way to be cleansed from the sins of our fathers as well. God told Israel that if they should find themselves in captivity and bondage that: "If they shall confess their iniquity, *and the iniquity of their fathers,* with their trespass which they trespassed against me and that also they have walked contrary unto me. . .then will I remember my covenant with Jacob. . .and Isaac. . .and Abraham." God gave these instructions. In later years, Nehemiah (Nehemiah 1:1-7), Daniel (Daniel 9:16), Jeremiah (Lamentations 5:7) and Hezekiah (II Chronicles 29:6) all found deliverance in times of captivity by confessing their own sin and the sins of their fathers. It is particularly important to confess the sins of your fathers (and mothers) if you learn that your ancestors have been involved in the occult, false religions, divorce, unforgiveness, drugs, and alcohol abuse, etc.

filled life. They are (1) knowing God personally, (2) obeying Him, (3) being thankful for everything, (4) being honest with yourself, with God, and with others, (5) resolving all differences with others God's way, (6) knowing and accepting God's purpose for your life and learning what He has done to fulfill his purpose in you, and (7) living for others rather than for yourself.

By fulfilling these seven prerequisites consistently, an individual can be filled with God's Spirit minute by minute. God will continuously channel His love, joy, peace, patience, gentleness, goodness, faith, meekness and self-control in and through that individual. It is available for you! Do you want to learn how to get a happy, successful Christian life for yourself so you can pass it along to your children? Learn the seven prerequisites for a happy, successful Christian life—and start applying them.

STEP ONE - KNOWING GOD

Having God's presence and power revealed in and through a person's life depends on knowing who God really is and learning what He wants to do for His people. As an individual's real knowledge of God increases, he will be able to trust God more and more. As faith grows, the joy and peace produced by God's presence will also grow. God's Word promises:

> Grace and peace be multiplied unto you *through the knowledge of God and of Jesus our Lord.* According as his divine power hath given unto us all things that pertain unto life and godliness, through the knowledge of him that hath called us to glory and virtue (II Peter 1:2-3).

The more a person knows about God the more that He can be trusted in any situation. The first step is learning about God, His attributes, His purposes and His promises. These things must be learned intellectually from the Bible first. Then as God is trusted to do and be what He promises, God's presence and His provision will actually be experienced in day-to-day living.

To start the process, there are ten basic facts about God which must be accepted. They are: (1) He is, (2) He is all-powerful, (3) He is all-knowing, (4) He is everywhere, (5) He is in absolute and total control of all things. Nothing can

happen unless He either causes it or permits it, (6) He is all
good so that He will bring good out of everything no matter
how tragic it may appear, (7) He proved His love for us
when He died on the cross for our sins, (8) He never
changes, (9) He, therefore, is loving us *right now*, and (10)
Because of all He is and the fact that He is loving us *right
now,* He can be trusted completely in every situation.

God has revealed these facts and many others about
Himself in the Bible. Since facts must be known before they
can be a benefit to us, we must grow in our knowledge of the
Lord by studying the Bible. As our intellectual knowledge
of the Lord grows, we can trust Him more. As we believe, He
will do those things we are trusting Him for and He will
make them real in our experience. As He reveals Himself in
our lives, we can actually know Him in a real and personal
way. It starts once we believe and trust that the Lord Jesus
is indeed God and that He actually took all of our personal
sins when He went to the cross. As we believe, the risen
Christ will come into our hearts and give us a new life.

If we really know God and know Him to be all that He is,
the next two prerequisites for a happy, successful Christian
life should come naturally.

STEP TWO - OBEDIENCE

If God is all the Bible says He is, then He should be
obeyed in all things without question. His presence and
power are promised to those who obey Him. In Acts 5:29-32
the Apostle Peter said:

> We ought to obey God rather than men. The god of our fathers
> raised up Jesus, whom ye slew and hanged on a tree. Him hath
> God exalted with his right hand to be a Prince and a Saviour,
> for to give repentance to Israel, and forgiveness of sins. And we
> are his witnesses of these things; and so is also the Holy Ghost
> whom God hath given to them that obey him.

When we obey God, the third person of the Trinity, the
Holy Spirit, fills us. The presence and power of God is
thereby manifested in our lives. We experience and enjoy
the fruit which God's Spirit produces. This fruit is love,
joy, peace, patience, gentleness, goodness, faithfulness,
meekness, and self control. Along with this "fruit of the
Spirit" God also promises a host of other blessings to those

who obey. They include health (Exodus 15:26), blessings from heaven (Malachi 3:10), and provision of material needs (Matthew 6:25, 33).

To obey God and enjoy His blessings, we must know what He wants. His will is revealed to us as we carefully and regularly study His word.

STEP THREE - A THANKFUL HEART

One of God's commands is to be thankful in every situation and every circumstance. In I Thessalonians 5:18 God says:

> In every thing give thanks: for this is the will of God in Christ Jesus concerning you.

The Bible reveals God to be all knowing---all powerful---all wise---all loving---and in total and absolute control of every situation. If God is all the Bible says He is, then we can thank Him for every situation in which we find ourselves. No one should worry or fret or fear in any circumstance. Instead, we should share our cares and burdens with Him in prayer *with thanksgiving*. In Philippians 4:6-7 God says:

> Be careful (anxious) for nothing; but in every thing by prayer and supplication *with thanksgiving* let your requests be made known unto God. And the peace of God, which passeth all understanding, shall keep your hearts and minds through Christ Jesus.

How can we be thankful in everything? Only by faith. Instead of looking at circumstances, we must look at the loving God who is in control of the circumstances.

Why can we be thankful in everything? Because the all-powerful, all-knowing, all-loving, all-good God who is in total and absolute control of all things has told us:

> ...that all things work together for good to them that love God, to them who are the called according to his purpose (Romans 8:28).

God does not promise that all things will be good. However, He does promise that He will work all things together and bring good out of them. For that reason we can thank Him for every situation, every irritation, and every tragedy, knowing that He has permitted it---and will bring good out of it.

STEP FOUR - BEING HONEST
WITH YOURSELF, GOD, AND OTHERS

Sin can be divided into three categories or types. The three happiness-robbers are wrong attitudes, wrong actions, and fears. These happiness-destroyers stem from not really trusting God in every situation. Most people see that actions which are contrary to God's law are sin. Recognizing that wrong attitudes or failing to trust God is also sin is sometimes more difficult.

Guilty feelings, wrong attitudes, and fear are "happiness-destroyers." They keep us from enjoying the happy, successful life God gives when He is free to manifest His power and presence in us continually. Each of us is subject to these happiness-destroyers. Some learn to live or "exist" with guilt, wrong attitudes, or fears. God, however, has provided a way of deliverance from them. His promise is given in I John 1:9, which says:

> If we confess our sins, he is faithful and just to forgive us our sins, and to cleanse us from all unrighteousness.

In this verse God promises not only forgiveness but *cleansing* when we agree with Him about our sin. That is what confession really is---agreeing with God. Truly seeing our sin as God sees it is the door to forgiveness and cleansing. In the verse which follows, the Apostle John says that confession of sin is needed regularly by all of us because. . .

> If we say that we have not sinned, we make him a liar, and his word is not in us (I John 1:10).

When we get honest about sin, the blood of Jesus Christ shed on Calvary's cross will cleanse it away. When we have been cleansed, there is nothing to hinder the Holy Spirit from filling us. He then manifests His love, joy, peace, patience, gentleness, goodness, faith, meekness, and self-control in us and through us.

STEP FIVE - RESOLVING DIFFERENCES
GOD'S WAY

Unresolved differences and hurts which have never been healed or made right, poison lives. They are often deep-rooted and are frequently covered up. Even though they may be denied, unresolved differences produce bitterness. They damage health. They keep the Spirit of God from manifesting His power and presence in individuals, their families, and their churches. Resolving such differences in God's way is essential for living the happy, successful Christian life. In Matthew 18:15 God tells what to do when someone offends:

> Moreover if thy brother shall trespass against thee, go and tell him his fault between thee and him alone: if he shall hear thee, thou hast gained thy brother.

That verse is probably the most ignored passage in the Bible. Look at it carefully. When someone offends you, you must not talk to anyone else about the problem. The proper approach is to go to the one who has offended you, *acknowledging that you are wrong to feel bitterness and hurt over the offense.* Explain why you are troubled. Ask the other party to forgive you for the way you feel. Ask him to pray for you to get victory over your feelings. In ninety-nine cases out of one-hundred if you have gone with a right attitude, the offender will forgive you. Normally he will also seek to right the wrong he has committed. (If you know that you have offended someone else, Matthew 5:23-24 says you must go to the one you offended. Whether, therefore, you are offended or the offender, whenever things are not right with another person, you must seek to right the wrong.)

In the rare situation when the difference cannot be resolved between the two parties concerned, Matthew 18:16 sets forth the next step. It says:

> But if he will not hear thee, then take with thee one or two more, that in the mouth of two or three witnesses every word may be established.

The two or three witnesses (not just someone who will agree automatically with you) try to help the two parties see the truth. If they cannot, the matter must be brought before the entire church (or body) concerned to resolve the difference. Matthew 18:17 sets forth the procedure:

> And if he shall neglect to hear them, tell it unto the church: but if he neglect to hear the church, let him be unto thee as an heathen man and a publican.

The party or parties which will not accept the judgment
of the church (or body) concerned are to be put away. They
are to be treated as if they were not Christians. God wants
unity among His people and in His church. He wants this
oneness, for it is the pathway to seeing His power and
presence manifested among them. Things we try to ignore
and finally "get over" are not resolved God's way. When
covered-up, differences leave scars which cause deep-down
trouble for years. However, once the differences are resolved, He promises that His people can use His power and
authority (Matthew 18:18), that they will have unbelievable
power in prayer (Matthew 18:19), and that He will be with
them (Matthew 18:20).

STEP SIX - JOYOUS LIVING
KNOWING GOD'S PURPOSE FOR
YOUR LIFE

A drifting, aimless, goalless life can be neither successful
nor satisfying. To be happy, man needs goals. He also
needs to be making progress toward accomplishing them.

At various stages of life, goals may be mainly physical:
learning to walk, eat, achieving sports skills, etc. Early
educational goals such as learning to read are followed by
the goal of going to junior high, high school graduation,
and earning special honors or a college scholarship. A job
brings a whole new set of goals. Learning skills, earning
promotions, getting bigger paychecks all create interest
and give an individual something for which to strive.
Others get their hearts set on a car, clothes, a wife or
husband, and a home. Goals drive us to work to accomplish
them.

Ultimately, horizons must broaden. Goals which are
purely physical or material cannot satisfy for long. Some
will seek fulfillment in the family. Others will gain satisfaction from politics, exercising power, travel, and church
work or community service. To be happy---to prevent
stagnation---man needs to achieve. The Bible says:

...the desire accomplished is sweet to the soul (Proverbs 13:19).

Achieving educational, financial, or family goals, however, cannot fully satisfy. For true blessedness, a person
must be working towards accomplishing some goals in the

spiritual realm. The Bible speaks to those who have accomplished worldly goals and ambitions but are not truly satisfied. In Haggai 1:5-7, the Word of God says:

> Now therefore thus saith the Lord of hosts; Consider your ways. Ye have sown much, and bring in little; ye eat, but ye have not enough; ye drink, but ye are not filled with drink; ye clothe you, but there is none warm; and he that earneth wages earneth wages to put it into a bag with holes. Thus saith the Lord of hosts; Consider your ways.

These verses picture the age in which we live. People today have things but little real happiness. To know true happiness and fulfillment which the Bible calls "blessedness," a person must have spiritual goals. His spiritual goals must line up with God's goals for his life.

God has a plan for man. It is revealed in His Word---the Bible. In Genesis 1:26-27 He records His original plan for man.

> And God said, Let us make man in our image, after our likeness: and let them have dominion over the fish of the sea, and over the fowl of the air, and over the cattle, and over all the earth, and over every creeping thing that creepeth upon the earth. So God created man in his own image, in the image of God created he him; male and female created he them.

God made man to be like Himself. God wanted someone He could love and someone with whom he could fellowship. A holy, pure, reasoning, feeling, intelligent God needed beings like Himself with whom to share His life and world. Therefore, He made man. He made him in His own image. Man was a living soul with a spirit. Like God, he had the ability to think, feel, and make decisions. He was placed in the center of God's perfect creation and given charge over it. All was good and perfect.

Things did not stay that way long. Man used his free will to rebel against God. He succumbed to Satan's temptation. When man sinned, he lost the purity which made him like God. His spirit, in so far as it was able to commune with God, died. Being dead spiritually, man lost the capacity to fellowship with God, who is Spirit.

Man not only sinned---he became a sinner by nature. Since then all men have been born with the image of Adam. No man since has had to be taught to do wrong. It just

comes naturally. A second result of man's fall into sin was
the change in who controlled the earth. God gave man
dominion over the earth. Man chose to follow Satan rather
than the God who made him. As a result, Satan got control
of man and also of the earth that God had placed under
man's dominion. The New Testament says:

> Wherein in time past ye walked according to the course of this
> world, according to the prince of the power of the air, the spirit
> that now worketh in the children of disobedience: Among
> whom also we all had our conversation in times past in the
> lusts of our flesh, fulfilling the desires of the flesh and of the
> mind; and were by nature the children of wrath, even as others
> (Ephesians 2:2-3).

God's great plan and purpose for man in the world was
thwarted by Satan's appeal to man's lust, appetites, and
pride. Man and the world were both ruined in the process.
As a result of one man's sin, death and all of the other
results of sin came into God's perfect universe. They have
plagued everyone born since. The world is in a mess today
because Satan controls the world's people. However, God is
not to be thwarted.

The Scripture tells us that God is all-powerful and all-
knowing. What He sets out to do, He accomplishes. Read
this passage from Psalm 33:

> By the word of the Lord were the heavens made; and all the host
> of them by the breath of his mouth. He gathereth the waters of
> the sea together as an heap: he layeth up the depth in
> storehouses. Let all the earth fear the Lord: let all the inhabi-
> tants of the world stand in awe of him. For He spake and it was
> done; he commanded, and it stood fast.

> The Lord bringeth the counsel of the heathen to nought: he
> maketh the devices of the people of none effect. *The counsel
> [plan] of the Lord standeth for ever,* the thoughts of his heart to
> all generations. Blessed is the nation whose god is the Lord;
> and the people whom he hath chosen for his own inheritance.

The counsel or plan of the Lord stands forever no matter
what man or Satan may do. Today God is fulfilling His
original plan to make man in His own image through Jesus
Christ.

> But God, who is rich in mercy, for his great love wherewith he
> loved us, Even when we were dead in sins, hath quickened us

together with Christ, (by grace ye are saved:) And hath raised us up together and made us sit together in heavenly places in Christ Jesus: That in the ages to come he might shew the exceeding riches of his grace in his kindness toward us through Christ Jesus. For by grace are ye saved through faith; and that not of yourselves it is the gift of God; Not of works, lest any man should boast (Ephesians 2:4-9).

The Lord Jesus---God dwelling in human flesh---came to earth to die in man's place. He came to pay the penalty God imposed for sin from the beginning. When man sinned, man came under a death penalty. God had said:

The soul that sinneth it shall die...the wages of sin is death (Ezekiel 18:3; Romans 6:23).

Because all men are sinners, they are therefore under sentence of physical death and they are already spiritually dead also. Those who die with their sins will have to be separated from God forever in Hell. However, God, who loves man, came in the person of the Lord Jesus Christ to pay man's sin debt. This He did when He shed His blood on the cross of Calvary.

He was buried and after three days in the tomb He arose! He came out of the grave to be the new life of those who would believe that He paid their sin debt and receive Him. This is the Gospel---the good news.

As the Lord Jesus through His Holy Spirit comes to live His resurrected life in men who receive Him, they become spiritually alive. Their spirit comes alive to God. They are able to communicate with Him. They now understand Him. They are born anew! From then on, everything which happens to them is part of God's plan for making them like Himself. The Scripture says:

And we know that all things work together for good to them that love God, to them who are the called *according to his purpose*. For whom he did foreknow, he also did predestinate to be conformed to the image of his Son that he might be the firstborn among many brethren (Romans 8:28-29).

To be conformed to the image of Christ is to be made like God, for the Lord Jesus is God in human flesh. He came to show us exactly what God is like. All of the New Testament points to this glorious fulfillment of God's original purpose for man. It happens as Christ lives His life through those who believe and receive Him.

In Galatians 1:15-16, the Apostle Paul pointed to the fulfillment of the divine purpose in himself when he wrote:

> . . .it pleased God who separated me from my mother's womb, and called me by his grace, *To reveal his Son in me,* that I might preach Him among the heathen.

Christ lives in all those who receive Him as Saviour. However, His life does not show in many Christians. Their problem is that they have not really understood all that happened at Calvary when the Lord Jesus died for us. The Apostle Paul pointed to the rest of what God did to conform us to Christ when he wrote:

> I am crucified with Christ: nevertheless I live; yet not I, but Christ liveth in me: and the life which I now live in the flesh I live by the faith of the Son of God, who loved me and gave himself for me. (Galatians 2:20)

Christ died for me, and my old life---the life I got from Adam---died with Him also. Paul wrote:

> Knowing this, that our old man is crucified with him, that the body of sin might be destroyed, that henceforth we should not serve sin. (Romans 6:6)

The truth is presented in many places in the New Testament. When we are baptized (immersed), we are picturing, "I believe Christ died for me and rose again. *And* also my old life died with Him and was buried and I have been raised again to a new life in Him."

Of course, even though *Christ is in us if we have received Him and even though we are being conformed to His image,* He may not be clearly seen sometimes because. . .

> ....we have this treasure [Christ and his Holy Spirit] in earthen vessels [our flesh] (II Corinthians 4:7).

The Lord Jesus lives in our bodies of flesh which can still sin. Sin keeps Christ from being clearly seen in us now. However, we shall be like Him when He comes again---or when we go to be with Him at the time of physical death. The Apostle John, writing to those who had received Christ as Saviour, says:

> Beloved, now are we the sons of God, and it doth not yet appear

what we shall be: but we know that when he shall appear, we shall be like him; for we shall see him as he is. And every man that hath this hope in him purifieth himself, even as he is pure (I John 3:2-3).

This is our hope. To be like the Lord Jesus Christ is the only truly satisfying spiritual goal in life. All people do not have this hope. All of us are God's creatures but all of us are not God's children. Only those who have been born again are being conformed to His image. The Scripture says:

He came unto his own, and his own received him not. But as many as received him, to them gave he power to become the sons of God, even to them that believe on his name: which were born, not of blood, nor of the will of the flesh, nor of the will of man, but of God (John 1:11-13).

Have you seen that you are a sinner? Have you seen that you are deserving of Hell? Have you seen that Christ died in your place and rose again? Have you asked Him into your heart to be your Saviour and Lord and Life? If so, you can know that you have eternal life and that you are saved. The Scripture says:

He that hath the Son hath life; and he that hath not the Son of God hath not life. These things have I written unto you that believe [trust] on the name of the Son of God; that ye may know that ye have eternal life (I John 5:12-13).

If you are not sure that the Lord Jesus is living in you, will you invite Him into your heart to be your Saviour and Lord *right now?* If you believe that Jesus is God and that He will save you if you ask Him, do it right now in your heart and with your lips. In your own words, or with the words which follow, tell the Lord:

Lord, I know that I am a sinner. I deserve to be separated from you and be punished forever in Hell. I believe, however, that you paid for all my sins when you went on the cross and shed your blood. I thank you for dying for me. Please come into my heart right now and live there forever as my Lord and Saviour. I thank you in Jesus' Name for doing it.

If you have believed and opened your heart to the Lord Jesus, you can be assured that He now is living in you. Thank Him, right now, for saving you. You can have this assurance for He has said:

Behold, I stand at the door and knock: if any man hear my voice, and open the door, *I will come in to him,* and will sup with him, and he with me (Revelation 3:20).

If you in simple faith came to the Lord Jesus in prayer believing that He died for you, you can be assured that He did not turn you away. He has promised:

. . .him that cometh to me I will in no wise cast out (John 6:37).

Once you have believed and invited the Lord Jesus into your heart, you can be assured that He will never leave you. He has said:

I will never leave thee, nor forsake thee (Hebrews 13:5).

Once you have trusted the Lord Jesus to save you, He wants you to confess Him before others. He says:

Whosoever therefore shall confess me before men, him will I confess also before my Father which is in heaven (Matthew 10:32).

Our confession before men should be made in two ways. The Lord Jesus told a man whom He had saved:

Go home to thy friends, and tell them how great things the Lord hath done for thee, and hath had compassion on thee (Mark 5:19).

You should also tell friends and loved ones that you have been saved. Some will rejoice. Some will be interested in how they can be saved. Others will not understand immediately.*

The second way that we confess publicly what the Lord Jesus has done for us is by being baptized in water. Through baptism, we picture that Jesus died, was buried and rose again to take away our sin. As we are immersed in water we are also testifying that our old life was crucified with the Lord Jesus, that we were buried with Him, and

---

*If you have trusted Christ as a result of reading this book, please write to me so I can rejoice with you. I promise to pray regularly for you. Write to me: John Stormer, Box 32, Florissant, Mo. 63032 and I will send you some materials to help you start your new life in Christ.

that we have been raised to a new life in Christ.

The Scriptures show clearly that we should be baptized as soon as we believe. Notice in the following verses that everyone who was baptized believed first. See Acts 2:22-41, 8:12-13, 8:26-39, 9:3-18, 16:13-15, 16:25-34 and 18:8.

Once we have confessed our salvation to men with our mouths and by baptism, we are commanded to meet regularly with other Christians in a Bible-believing church. The Bible says that we are not to be. . .

> . . . forsaking the assembling of ourselves together as the manner of some is (Hebrews 10:25).

Daily Bible study is essential for spiritual growth. God's Word says:

> Man shall not live by bread alone, but by every word that proceedeth out of the mouth of God. . .As newborn babes desire the sincere milk of the word, that ye may grow thereby.....Study to shew thyself approved unto God, a workman that needeth not to be ashamed, rightly dividing [applying] the word of truth (Matthew 4:4, I Peter 2:2, II Timothy 2:15).

Read the Gospel of St. John first. Follow with the first Epistle of John, Romans, Mark, Luke, Ephesians, Philippians, Colossians, Matthew and on through the New Testament. Read some Psalms every day---and develop the habit of reading one chapter of Proverbs daily as well. Before reading the Bible, ask the Holy Spirit to show you what it means. Pray as the writer of Psalm 119 did when he cried out to God and said:

> Open thou mine eyes that I may behold wondrous things out of thy law (Psalm 119:18).

As the scriptures are studied, God will show what He expects step by step. As knowledge of Him and His ways grows, obey Him. Be thankful. Confess sin whenever there is disobedience. Resolve differences with others God's way. Seek to be like the Lord Jesus and live for others. That should be the purpose and goal of our life.

STEP SEVEN - LIVING FOR OTHERS

Once the Lord Jesus comes into the heart of an individual, he or she is saved. God then starts working to make the new Christian like the Lord Jesus. One way to be like

Christ is to live your life by meeting the needs of others
rather than living for self. The Lord Jesus gave the
commandment to live for others just before He went to the
Cross. He said:

> This is my commandment, That ye love one another, as I have
> loved you. Greater love hath no man than this, that a man lay
> down his life for his friends. (John 15:12-13)

He has already given us the example to follow. He
actually gave His life. At the Last Supper, the Lord Jesus
showed how our lives can be "laid down." After eating He
laid aside His garments, took a bason, water and a towel
and washed His disciples' feet. When He finished, he said
unto them:

> Know ye what I have done to you? Ye call me Master and Lord
> and ye say well: for so I am. If I then, your Lord and Master,
> have washed your feet; ye also ought to wash one another's
> feet. For I have given you an example, that ye should do as I
> have done to you. Verily, verily, I say unto you, the servant is
> not greater than his lord; neither he that is sent greater than he
> that sent him. *If ye know these things, happy are ye if ye do
> them.* (John 13:12b-17)

Living to meet the needs of others rather than living for
self is the way of true happiness. Jesus said it. Do you
believe it? Will you do it: If you follow this blueprint, God's
presence and power will be revealed in you and ultimately
in the lives of your children. Remember: your children will
be what you are!

Chapter X

YOU WILL BE
WHAT YOUR CHURCH IS

> *Let us hold fast the profession of our faith without
> wavering; (for he is faithful that promised;) And let us
> consider one another to provoke [stimulate] unto love and
> to good works; not forsaking the assembling of ourselves
> together as the manner of some is; but exhorting one
> another; and so much the more, as ye see the day
> approaching.*
>
> *—Hebrews 10:23-25*

FINDING THE CHURCH God wants you to attend
should be the first goal for a new Christian. Deciding to
attend regularly and faithfully is the most important single
decision in life once a person has been saved by receiving
Christ.

What a person becomes as a Christian will be largely
determined by the church that he attends. Therefore, the
right church is vitally important. Consider how a church
shapes lives:

If the church is doctrinally sound, the new Christian will be
taught and will learn sound Bible doctrine.

If the church emphasizes soul-winning, the new Christian's
concern for lost people will grow. The know-how to help them
find Christ will be learned through the preaching of a godly
pastor and the example of faithful believers.

If the church teaches holy living, and how to use the Bible to
establish godly standards for dress and appearance, amusements, habits, customs, etc. the new Christian will be trained
and challenged to build Biblical standards in his life, home and
family.

If the church is controlled by love and the members "love one another as Christ loved the church and gave himself for it," the new Christian will be loved and will learn to love and do the works of love.

If God's power is being manifested through the lives of the pastor and people, the new Christian will be challenged also to seek to have God's power in his own life.

If the church does the Biblical job of "perfecting the saints for the work of the ministry," the new Christian will find himself being challenged and trained to do God's work in the church and in the community.

If the church administers the ordinances of baptism and the Lord's Supper Biblically and safeguards their meaning, the new Christian will never forget the new life received by trusting Christ and the need to live a holy life in fellowship and communion with the Lord and His people.

If the church operates a Christian day school or strongly supports a school operated by another Bible-believing church, the church is likely to be concerned about the Christian growth and development of all of the children in the church.

How a church measures up in most of these areas can be quickly determined by observation. How sound the church is doctrinally demands special scrutiny. It is essential that the pastor, the church itself, and any organizations with which it is affiliated hold to the sound doctrines of the Word of God and teach them. This insures that members of the church will . . .

. . . . henceforth be no more children, tossed to and fro, and carried about with every wind of doctrine, by the sleight of men, and cunning craftiness, whereby they lie in wait to deceive (Ephesians 4:14).

To determine whether a church is sound in doctrine and practice, ask the pastor and/or the leaders of the church (Sunday school teachers, etc.) these questions:

Are *all* of the Words in the Bible God's Words? Is the Bible totally and completely true and without any errors or mistakes? (See II Timothy 3:16-17.)

Did God make the world and everything in it including man in six actual days—resting on the seventh? (See Genesis 1:1-2:3.)

Was Jesus Christ miraculously conceived by the Holy Spirit and actually born of a virgin? (See Matthew 1:18-25 and Luke 1:26-38.)

Is Jesus Christ God? (See John 1:1,14; 10:30; and 14:7-9.)

Was it necessary for the Lord Jesus to die on the cross and shed His blood to pay for man's sin? (See Hebrews 9:22.)

Did the Lord Jesus actually arise from the dead, coming out of the tomb *bodily* on the third day (not just in Spirit)? (See Luke 24:36-45.)

Are Heaven and Hell real places with Heaven having streets of gold and Hell being a place of torment with real flames which will burn forever? (See Revelation 20:10-15 and 21:21.)

If a person dies without being born again by believing and receiving Christ as Saviour, will he burn forever in Hell? (See John 14:6; Revelation 20:10-15 and Mark 9:42-48.)

Can a person be saved by faith in Jesus Christ *alone* without adding baptism, good works, church membership, etc. to his faith? (See Ephesians 2:8-9; Titus 3:5; and John 14:6.)

Even though a person can be saved without these things should he be baptized, join a church, and do good works once he is saved? (See Mathew 28:18-20; Hebrews 10:25 and Ephesians 2:10.)

Once a person has been saved by trusting Jesus Christ is he saved forever even though he may sin and fail sometimes? (See John 6:37 and 10:27-29.)

Will Jesus Christ take all of His saved people out of the world before the seven year time of great trouble when the Anti-Christ will rule over the world? (See I Thessalonians 4:13-18 and II Thessalonians 2:1-12.)

Do you believe that after this seven years, the Lord Jesus will come back to earth with His people, put down all wickedness and rule and reign over the earth for 1000 years? (See Revelation 20:1-6.)

If there is agreement with all of these truths, do all of the denominations, associations, fellowships or conventions the church is affiliated with hold to them, teach them in their schools, etc.? (See Amos 3:3.)

If a church is sound doctrinally, all of these questions will be answered with a strong "Yes." There are a few other questions which should be answered with a definite "No." They include:

Does anyone in a leadership position in your church (or any organization with which your church is affiliated) have doctrinal views differing from these sound Bible positions you profess? (See Amos 3:3 and Acts 20:26-31.)

Do you believe that a person has to speak in "tongues" to be saved or to show that he is filled with the Holy Spirit? (See I Corinthians 12:4-11, 29-31 and 13:8-10.)

Can anyone pray or get blessings from God by going through anyone other than the Lord Jesus Christ? (See I Timothy 2:5.)

Does your church teach or believe that any book, writings, or teachings other than the Bible are inspired by God and therefore equal to the Bible? (See Revelation 22:18-19.)

Do baptism, the Lord's Supper or church membership help a person to be saved or help to keep them saved? (See Romans 6:23 and Ephesians 2:8-9.)

Does your church permit women to be preachers? (See I Corinthians 14:34 and I Timothy 2:11-12.)

Is your church or your denomination (if your church is not completely independent) a part of the liberal, Bible-denying National or World Councils of Churches? (See II Corinthians 6:14-7:1.)

If a church and its leaders cannot answer "Yes" to the first set of questions and "No" to the second, they have departed in some way from sound Bible doctrine and practice.

A church can be completely sound in doctrine and still fail to be a true, *living* New Testament body of believers. Several additional tests are needed. In His Word, God says that the function of the church and the leaders whom He puts in the church is. . .

. . .the perfecting of the saints for the work of the ministry, for the edifying of the body of Christ. (Ephesians 4:12)

The church is the institution that God established to win the lost *and* to teach them to do the work of the ministry.

There are seven facets to the "work of the ministry." They are illustrated by the seven activities performed by the Lord Jesus in Mark 1:14-41 as He started His ministry. The "work of the ministry" includes (1) winning lost people by giving them the Gospel, (2) calling them to follow Jesus in God's service, (3) teaching them, (4) helping those afflicted by Satan and his evil spirits, (5) ministering to the sick, (6) the ministry of prayer and (7) having compassion toward those who have spiritual, emotional or physical needs.

The "right" church does not just teach doctrine and ways

to minister. It also provides fellowship and an atmosphere where church members are encouraged to put into practice what they have been taught. Hebrews 10:23-25 says that once we have been saved:

> Let us hold fast the profession of our faith without wavering; (for he is faithful that promised;) And let us consider one another to provoke unto love and to good works: Not forsaking the assembling of ourselves together as the manner of some is; but exhorting one another: and so much the more, as ye see the day approaching.

In a true New Testament church, everyone in the body of believers has a dependence upon the others in the body and a responsibility to help others live God's way. Explosions can result, however, as efforts are made to help a fellow believer see his needs to be more loving, to resolve differences God's way, to put finances on a Biblical basis, to do good works, etc. People resent having faults pointed out or being told what they should be doing.

That is why the Bible teaches that the way to bring fellow believers to face needs and grow stronger in faith is by. . .

. . .speaking the truth *in love* (Ephesians 4:15).

The mark of a true New Testament church is love. The Lord Jesus said:

> A new commandment I give unto you, That ye love one another; as I have loved you, that ye also love one another. By this shall all men know that ye are my disciples, if ye have love one to another. (John 13:34-35)

Christians in New Testament times were shown to be true disciples or followers of the Lord Jesus, not by their doctrine or their zeal, but by their love. Love makes all of the other functions of the church work. People will accept advice, help, correction, instruction, and challenges to work from those that they know truly love them. Therefore in seeking a church, find one where the people are controlled by love for the Lord and for one another.

As contradictory as it may seem, a loving church must also be a warring church. The Bible says:

> Ye that love the Lord, hate evil (Psalm 97:10).

A church which truly stands for the Bible must actively

oppose evils such as abortion, drugs, alcohol, communism
and socialism, immorality, pornography, homosexuality,
the occult, etc. However, even as it stands against these
evils, the church must be careful to remember that the
battle is not against the individuals who are promoting the
evil. The war is with Satan and the forces of darkness.
Ephesians 6:12 identifies the real enemy, saying. . .

> . . .we wrestle not against flesh and blood, but against
> principalities, against powers, against the rulers of the dark-
> ness of this world, against spiritual wickedness in high places.

These four categories of spiritual forces control and
promote wickedness in the world by influencing and controlling individuals. The "right church" will, therefore,
hate evil and war against it. At the same time, it will love
and try to win individuals involved in the sin and wickedness to the Lord.

Summing up: The right church will be sound in doctrine.
It will promote holy living. Its people will be trained and
challenged to do the work of the ministry. The members will
manifest willingness to minister to one another and be
ministered to in areas of weakness. Above all, the church
will be controlled and motivated by love. Even as it loves,
however, it will be warring against wickedness.

All of these functions will result from continual, consistent preaching of God's Word. The Apostle Paul told
Timothy. . .

> Till I come, give attendance to reading, to exhortation, to
> doctrine (I Timothy 4:13).

In a true New Testament church, the pastor should read
the Scriptures, and explain them to the people. This is done
through verse-by-verse, chapter-by-chapter, book-by-book
teaching of the Bible. In addition there must also be
exhortation. This is strong preaching in which the congregation is challenged to apply in their lives what they have
been taught. Reading and exhortation is followed by
doctrine. Doctrine is teaching which shows how the verse-
by-verse teaching and the life applications fit into God's
overall scheme of things as revealed in the entire Bible.

"Attend the church of your choice this Sunday" is a
popular slogan. It is not a Scriptural concept. Rather than

attending the church "of your choice," make sure you attend the church "of God's choice."

To be sure of attending the church of God's choice, be like the people described in Acts 17:10-12. The Apostle Paul came to a town in Greece called Berea. He had just been driven out of a town called Thessalonica. As he preached to the Bereans, the Scriptures tell of their reactions:

> These were more noble than those in Thessalonica, in that they received the word with all readiness of mind, and searched the scriptures daily, whether those things were so. Therefore many of them believed.

Be a Berean. Commit yourself to finding a church which meets the test of Biblical standards. Then attend it faithfully. This is vitally important, for you will be what your church is; and what you are, your children will be.

Chapter XI

STABLE, SECURE HOMES
PRODUCE HAPPY CHILDREN

> *From the beginning of the creation God made them male
> and female. For this cause shall a man leave his father and
> mother, and cleave to his wife; and they twain shall be one
> flesh: so then they are no more twain, but one flesh. What
> therefore God hath joined together, let not man put
> asunder.*
>
> *--Mark 10:6-9*

I HELPED TO MARRY A FINE YOUNG COUPLE a number of years ago. As the other preacher and I were waiting in his study for the ceremony to start, he said, "You know---it's come to the point where I'd rather have a funeral than a wedding." He explained, "When you bury someone it stays done."

He was not being funny. He was not being crude. He was not being cynical. He was a deeply concerned man. For years he had counseled folks with marriage problems and then had seen them break up.

That troubled pastor approached another marriage ceremony with a real burden. He was questioning, "Are these two young people really serious? Are they really prepared to undertake the responsibilities of marriage? Are they committed to make it work---no matter what?"

His questions are valid. Divorce has reached the epidemic stage in America. It has happened during our lifetime. Consider these facts:

> In 1900 one out of 100 marriages ended in divorce. Today it is one out of two. The divorce rate has tripled since 1960.

In an article, *Too Many Divorces, Too Soon,* noted anthropologist, Margaret Mead, showed how selfishness and growing irresponsibility destroys half of all marriages ---and many of the children they produce. Writing in the February 1974 *Redbook* magazine, she said:

> In our generation divorce has become a part of the American way of life. . .We no longer deeply believe that two people who have made the choice to marry should necessarily try to weather the storms that shake any vital, intimate relationship. Instead, more and more, our answer to a difficulty in marriage is: Try it again with someone else.

All too often the motivation for changing marriage partners in such circumstances is the hope of finding someone who will please *me*---do things *my* way---meet *my* standards. If both husband and wife have this selfish, immature "me-first" attitude, someone is certain to be sadly disappointed. Miss Mead comments:

> Certainly this is not the point of view of two young people deeply in love for the first time. They enter marriage, however hurriedly, with the happy conviction that it will work, that they are different from those who fail. Some of them *are* different and *do* succeed magnificiently in growing into adulthood and parenthood serene and confident. But many do not---too many ---especially when there are children.

The arrival of a child often triggers the crisis. Immature young couples who have not really learned how to give themselves to "living for the other" cannot cope with the pressure a baby creates. Margaret Mead writes:

> Unprepared for parenthood, two young people who have become very close may see the new baby as an interloper. Or, if they are already restless, the baby may become just one more obstacle to pleasure and freedom. The mother is permanently stuck at home. The father is almost equally confined---or goes out alone. There is no money now for pleasure and almost nowhere the young couple can go for amusement with the baby. Then our current belief that a speedy divorce is the way out of the dilemma begins to take effect. . .each accuses the other of things they both fear and long for---freedom from responsibility, a chance to get away, longing for better opportunities in life, a way out of their unhealthy situation.

Couples who separate end up with deep hurts. When there

are children (and there are millions), they suffer the most. In addition to the millions who actually separate, many couples share a house and children but do not actually have a real home and marriage. Children from such families suffer in many of the same ways that children do whose parents actually separate. All these tragedies do not have to happen. They can be prevented.

Learning and applying seven basic concepts will enable any couple to build a happy, stable, secure home—a home which cannot be destroyed. These concepts are (1) The Bible is God's rulebook and instruction manual for marriage. (2) Marriage is a permanent, unbreakable union. (3) Marriage cannot be a 50-50 proposition. Each partner must fulfill his or her own responsibilities 100% whether the partner does or not. (4) Both the husband and wife must recognize they have distinctive personal needs which can be truly satisfied without guilt only in the marriage relationship. (5) At the same time both partners must be committed to recognizing and meeting their partner's needs which while different from their own are just as real and deeply felt. (6) All differences must be resolved God's way. (7) Recognize that a stable marriage must be based on trust and that a person can be trusted only as he or she is willing to trust another completely.

If even one partner in the marriage accepts and fulfills these concepts, the home cannot be destroyed. God will use the dedication of the partner who is fully committed to building a Christian home to transform the erring mate. Let's look at these seven principles in detail:

FOLLOW THE INSTRUCTIONS

God instituted marriage. Marriages fail when people try to live together by their own rules rather than God's. The cost is tragic. Homes break up. Lives are shattered. Loyalties are divided. Children get bruises that hurt all of their lives. Dreams of the bride and groom become nightmares. Sometimes the honeymoon ends in weeks or months. For others the trouble may build for years before the break comes.

About 450 marriages out of every 1000 now end in divorce. Contrast these tragic figures with the results of several surveys made in the United States and Canada in the last ten years. While one out of every two marriages end in divorce in the general population, only one out of fifty fails when the family regularly attends church together. Even more amazing, a nationwide survey found that only one out of 1525 marriages break up when both partners have trusted Jesus Christ as Saviour and Lord and faithfully follow His guidelines for life and marriage. A similar study showed the chances at one out of 1100. These studies indicate that chances for success and blessing in a truly Christian marriage are 600 to 700 times better than for those who try to do it the world's way.

There is a good reason. God established marriage. He gave us His rule book, the Bible. By following His instructions, we can succeed. By ignoring God's way, tragedy results. For success in any area of life, whether assembling a child's toy or building a marriage, read and follow the instructions.

To improve your chances in marriage by 550 times:

1. If you have not yet believed on the Lord Jesus Christ and received Him into your heart, do so right now. Read the Gospel of John and chapter IX of this book until you believe.

2. Get baptized. This is a testimony that your old life and way of doing things died with Christ and that you have been raised to a new life and way of living through His resurrected life in you.

3. Commit yourself personally to doing right. To find out what is right, start reading the Bible and praying regularly.

4. Read your Bible and pray every day with your partner and family.

5. Get active in a Christ-centered, Bible-preaching church. Attend every service, whether it is convenient or not. You will hear God's principles for living explained and be challenged to apply them.

6. Look for opportunities to serve the Lord together.

Salvation, faithful church attendance, personal Bible study, prayer, regular family devotions, and serving the Lord together multiply the chances for marriage success over 500 times. Successful marriages are stable marriages.

REAFFIRM YOUR PERMANENT COMMITMENT

Think back to when you made your marriage vows.

Almost everyone promises ". . .for better or worse. . . .till death do us part." This age-old part of the traditional marriage ceremony is based on Biblical concepts. Today, this promise for most people, if used at all, is just part of the formality of the marriage ritual. However, the Bible makes it very plain and definite that. . . .

> What therefore God hath joined together, let not man put asunder (Matthew 19:6).

God's Word also very plainly teaches that if a marriage does break up, there can be no remarriage. Those who do remarry commit an awful sin. The Lord Jesus said:

> Whosoever putteth away his wife, and marrieth another, committeth adultery: and whosoever marrieth her that is put away from her husband committeth adultery (Luke 16:18).

In Romans 7:2-3 God speaking through the Apostle Paul said:

> For the woman which hath an husband is bound by the law to her husband so long as he liveth; but if the husband be dead, she is loosed from the law of her husband. So then if, while her husband liveth, she be married to another man, she shall be called an adulteress: but if her husband be dead, she is free from that law; so that she is no adulteress, though she be married to another man.

Today's society has a very casual attitude toward God's commandments and a very shallow view of the importance of keeping promises. As a result, divorce rates are sky-rocketing. Often the ink is not dry on the divorce papers until one or both parties are remarried. Frequently they promise again ". . .for better or for worse. . .until death do us part. . . ."

Because people take their commitments very lightly, many marriages break up for very immature and silly reasons. Then the unresolved problems and conflicts and hurts from the first marriage often prevent the second or third from being really successful.*

----

*If you have been divorced and are already remarried, several steps are necessary to clear your own conscience and stabilize your present marriage. Problems and bitterness from a previous marriage will

Whether you are now in your first or second (or third or fourth) marriage, God wants to help you to make this marriage work. He wants to bless your union. He wants to use you *together* to be a blessing to one another, your children, and others. To give stability to your marriage and security to your partner, commit yourself now to stay married forever, *no matter what*. Make a further commitment to the Lord that even if your partner should leave you, you will never remarry.

Accepting God's standard for a permanent marriage relationship will make you determined and willing to resolve any difference no matter what it costs you. It will also drive you to your knees and to the Lord for the grace to do it.

Reaffirming your original and perhaps formal commitment to your partner is vitally important. Once you have prayerfully thought it through, sharing your "forever/ whatever" commitment will give your partner a sense of security --- and responsibility. If when you make this commitment, your partner does not get as excited as you do about its importance, do not get hurt or discouraged. Give God time to work on your spouse.

Once both partners have made the commitment, children should be told of it. In a day when children see the homes of many friends fall apart, knowing of your "forever/ whatever" commitment will give them a vitally important sense of security. It will also start building the foundations upon which they will someday approach marriage with the attitude that marriage is forever.

----

destroy or seriously mar your present marriage unless they are recognized, resolved, and removed. Face the events which led to your divorce and/or your reactions to them as sin. They need to be confessed to the Lord. Acknowledge to God that breaking your first marriage vows, your divorce and your remarriage were sins against Him. When you sincerely confess these sins to Him, He will forgive and cleanse you. You will sense a real release from the guilt (open or subconscious) which hinders you in making your present marriage stable and successful. Wrong attitudes toward your former partner must be corrected. Differences with former partners must be resolved. Forgiveness must be sought from God and your former partner for ways you were wrong in the first marriage. This will free you to receive God's blessing in your present marriage.

MARRIAGE IS NOT A 50-50 PROPOSITION

Vows, seriously taken, can keep a marriage together, but vows will not build a happy home. A home which is both secure and happy must be built on a real understanding of what makes a marriage successful.

The slogan "marriage is a 50-50 proposition" is heard frequently. It sounds logical. However, the logic behind it can destroy many marriages. The basis of a 50-50 marriage is, "If you will do your part, I will do mine." It leads to tragedy because there are times in every marriage when someone fails. In a 50-50 marriage, this causes the other partner to step back and refuse to do his 50%. Then the battle rages.

The 50-50 marriage is not God's way. The husband and wife who start marriage on a 50-50 basis will always be checking to see if the partner is fulfilling his or her 50%. When one partner falls short, bitterness results in the other. The partner who feels cheated will withold some of his 50% in an attempt to even the score. Things get worse. Even 90%-10% marriages will not work. The partner who is willing to give 90% will have a tendency to check to see if the partner is really fulfilling his or her 10%.

God's way in marriage is 100%-100%. Each partner is expected to give his or her 100% even if the other partner fails completely. If only *one* partner in the marriage faithfully gives his 100%, the home cannot be destroyed. God uses right actions and attitudes of the faithful one to straighten out and restore the failing partner.

God's instructions for the 100%-100% marriage are found in several places in the Bible. Ephesians 5:18-33 is the primary passage. In these verses, God gives each partner certain instructions. Both the husband and wife have different responsibilities assigned to them. In Ephesians 5:22-24, the wife is told:

> Wives submit yourselves unto your own husbands, as unto the Lord. For the husband is the head of the wife, even as Christ is the head of the church: and he is the saviour of the body. Therefore as the church is subject unto Christ, so let the wives be to their own husbands in every thing.

God does not qualify this instruction to the wife by

saying, "Submit. . .if your husband does right and fulfills
his responsibility." In fact, in a related passage in I Peter
3:1, the Lord says that a wife should fulfill her responsibilities without nagging, complaining, lecturing, or teaching
her husband. She will win him to the Lord's way by her
behavior. This wonderful promise says:

> Likewise, ye wives, be in subjection to your own husbands;
> that, if any obey not the word, they also may without the word
> be won by the conversation [behaviour] of the wives.

When a man fails to be what he should be in marriage,
God deals with him. Too often, however, the man does not
hear the Lord or feel the Lord's pressure because he is
already hearing his wife and feeling the pressure she is
applying. He can and will resist his wife's words, etc.
However, if she really lives I Peter 3:1 and is quiet and
sweet, submitting in all things, the man will feel God's
hand upon him. He may resist his wife, but he cannot resist
God for long.

The Bible teaches that the man is the head of the home.
This does not mean that the wife is inferior. The Lord is
careful to show us this in I Corinthians 11:3. He says:

> But I would have you know, that the head of every man is
> Christ; and the head of the woman is the man; and the head of
> Christ is God.

Being under authority is not a position of inferiority. This
verse reminds us that "the head of Christ is God." The Lord
Jesus is God and is equal with the Father in all ways. Yet
when He came to earth and became a man to die for our
sins, He submitted Himself to His heavenly Father in all
things. In submitting, He did not become inferior to His
Father in all things. However, He did all things because His
Father wanted it---and not just because He also wanted to.
God reminds us of this important truth in the very passage
where He tells us that "man is the head of the woman." God
has given this example to show that *submission is not a
mark of inferiority*. Every institution must have a head.
Otherwise anarchy results.

To avoid anarchy or a constant struggle over who is in
charge, God makes man the head of the family. However,
the man is not to be a dictator. In the verses which follow

the instructions to wives to submit, God severely limits the man's right to do anything he pleases. God, after giving the man the authority in the family, takes away his right to use it irresponsibly by telling him:

> Husbands, love your wives, even as Christ also loved the church, and gave himself for it (Ephesians 5:25).

Because of His love, the Lord Jesus gave everything, including His life, for His bride, the church. This is God's pattern for men in marriage. God does not tell the woman to submit *if* her husband loves her. God does not tell the man to love his wife, *if* she submits to him. In fact, by giving man his instructions using Christ's example, the husband is told to love his wife *even if* she should be in outright rebellion against him. The husband is *to love his wife as the Lord loved the church* and gave Himself for it. The Bible shows how the Lord loved. It says:

> But God commendeth [proved] his love toward us, in that, while we were yet sinners, Christ died for us...when we were enemies we were reconciled to God by the death of his son (Romans 5:8, 10).

Christ gave Himself for us (His bride) while we were yet sinners. We were actually enemies of God. Even so, He died for us. Seeing His love transforms our hearts and brings us to love Him. So, too, a husband's patient, longsuffering love will finally win the wife's heart and change her behavior. The Lord Jesus does not cleanse and perfect us by beating on us. He loves us and teaches us His Word! To see the full concept read Ephesians 5:25 with the two verses which follow. Ask God to give understanding of how the process works in marriage. The Bible says:

> Husbands, love your wives, even as Christ also loved the church, and gave himself for it; That he might sanctify and cleanse it with the washing of the water by the word, That he might present it to himself a glorious church, not having spot, or wrinkle, or any such thing; but that it should be holy without blemish.

There are no 50-50 arrangements in God's plan for a happy, successful marriage. Each partner is called upon to fulfill his or her own 100%. Each is responsible for his or her own 100% even if the other does nothing. This is not calling one partner or the other to life-long martyrdom. God will use the sweet, gentle, faithful submission of a wife to convict a wayward husband of his sin. Or, he can use the patient, undying Christ-like love and self-sacrifice of the husband to melt the hardened, rebellious heart of a straying wife. The techniques work not just to win the partner who is failing to fulfill his or her obligations. They will also effectively work to correct every little shortcoming a partner has.

It is impossible, humanly speaking, to give 100% without reacting to the failings of a partner. That is why the entire passage is introduced with the admonition:

> And be not drunk with wine, wherein is excess; *but be filled with the Spirit* (Ephesians 5:18).

As we are constantly being filled with God and His power and love (as following the steps in Chapter IX makes possible) we can be the husbands and wives He calls us to be.

When one partner (or the other) realizes that he has not been giving his own 100%, he should confess his failings to the Lord in detail. He should also ask his partner for forgiveness for failing to be the kind of mate God would have him to be. Do not go into detail on what you or your partner should be. Just seek forgiveness and then start submitting sweetly or loving the way that you should.

MEETING ONE ANOTHER'S NEEDS

Both the husband and the wife in a marriage have needs. Their needs are different, but the needs of both are very real. Unless these distinctive, individual needs are being satisfied within the marriage relationship, the security and stability of the home will be endangered.

Recognizing our own needs will. . .

> . . .safeguard us from drifting into a relationship where our needs are met outside of marriage—with all the tragedies that result.

A marriage breakup often occurs when someone outside the marriage begins to meet the basic emotional needs of one of the marriage partners. When this happens, the two people are drawn almost irresistibly to one another. Soon another marriage becomes a divorce statistic. Many fine people get caught in this trap without realizing why. They do not understand that the strong attraction they feel for someone other than their partner is just the result of the other person's meeting an emotional need which should be fulfilled by the marriage partner. When two people are meeting one another's basic emotional needs there is a strong and growing desire for a complete physical relationship. Recognizing our basic emotional need and seeing that it can be fulfilled without guilt only within the marriage relationship is vital protection against tragedy.

What are these basic emotional needs of the husband and wife?

God knows exactly what we need to be complete because He made us. In Ephesians 5:33, God tells husbands and wives how to meet the needs of their partners. He says:

> Nevertheless let every one of you in particular so love his wife even as himself; and the wife see that she reverence her husband.

A wife needs love. A husband needs to be respected and reverenced. A wife needs to hear that she is loved. A husband needs to know that his wife really thinks he is the greatest. A wife needs to receive regular evidence and reassurances of her husband's love. She needs and gets thrilled by little gifts, remembrances of important dates and events, and tokens of love. Of course, these assurances of love are empty and unsatisfying unless the husband also provides security, protection, needed maintenance on the home, etc. A husband deeply needs to be assured of his wife's respect, particularly when he fails in some way. A husband needs to know that his wife is dependent on him---just as Christ's bride, the church, is dependent on Him.

When the husband and wife do not recognize and work to meet the needs of their partners, grave dangers result. For example, a man who on the job is competent in accomplishing his assignments and is polite, courteous, and appreciative of the help of others will find a woman (particularly if she works for him) respecting him. Because the woman is meeting his need for respect, he will be drawn to her. He will start desiring to meet her needs.

Soon he will compare the respect of the woman on the job

with the nagging of his wife. The woman at the office or in
the plant does not know that he does not take out the
garbage and leaves his dirty socks or underwear on the
bathroom floor. The woman on the job will not point out his
failings (particularly if he is her boss) as his wife does. The
woman on the job is in danger also. She does not realize
that this very competent, appreciative man at work has all
of the same shortcomings of her own husband. In the
casual relationship at work (or wherever), these two people
do not have to share unpaid bills, sick children, the need for
a new washer, a second car, etc.* Without realizing it, soon
they find themselves meeting one another's basic needs.
The man at work will be supplying the attention and
kindness the woman needs. She will be giving the man the
respect he desires. Where two people are meeting these very
basic needs for love and respect, the desire for a complete
physical relationship becomes overpowering. Soon there is
another broken marriage. It is happening all of the time.

Recognizing your own basic need for reverence and
respect (the men) or love and attention (the women) is an
important safeguard against slipping into a relationship
where these needs are met outside of marriage.

MEETING YOUR PARTNER'S NEEDS

Recognizing our own basic need will also help us to
understand that our partner has needs which are just as
real and deeply felt as our own. This is vitally important.

Husbands cannot know from their own experiences how
much wives need to feel loved. They cannot really understand how wives need regular assurance and evidence of
that love. By the same token, wives cannot comprehend
how their husbands need reverence and respect.

About the only way a husband and wife will ever come to
realize that his or her partner has a real and deeply felt need
is to recognize his or her own personal need. By seeing and

----

*The pressure of bills, illness, unemployment, and debts are often seen
as the cause of divorce. Actually, if two people are really meeting one
another's basic needs for love and respect, they can face and solve these
problems of life together. In fact, in meeting them they are drawn even
closer together. When partners are not meeting one another's needs, the
marriage is in difficulty even if there are no health, financial, or family
pressures.

admitting how much he needs respect and reverence from his wife, a husband is prepared to understand that his wife also has a deeply felt need, which while different from his own, is very real. By the same token, the only way a wife can really experience or feel or share in the great need her husband has to be reverenced and respected is to recognize her own deep hunger for love and the assurance of it. Once she sees her own need, she is prepared to realize that her husband's need, while different, is just as deep and real. Coming to recognize our own emotional needs and seeing that our partners also have needs which are just as real and deeply felt will bring us to a willingness to give ourselves to meeting the needs of our partner. As we do so, God will see to it that they begin to meet out needs.

The real key to blessing in marriage is in making the goal of your life the meeting of the needs of your partner. In doing so, you will see your own needs met by God. In Luke 6:38 , the Lord Jesus said:

> Give, and it shall be given unto you; good measure, pressed down, and shaken together, and running over, shall men give into your bosom. For with the same measure that ye mete withal it shall be measured to you again.

Many people immediately think of money when they see or hear these instructions about giving. It does apply to finances, but there is a principle here which goes so much further than just money. God says, "Give and it shall be given unto you." In fact, He implies that we will receive much more than we give. This principle applies in every area of life. If we give love, we will get love. If we give help, we will get help. If we give encouragement, we get encouragement. If we give forgiveness to others, we will be forgiven. If we give a smile, we will get smiled at. The opposites apply also. If we hate, we will get hatred. Therefore, when we give ourselves to meeting the needs of others, we'll find others meeting our needs. Nowhere is this more true than in marriage.

When both partners are satisfying the needs of the other, they become more and more important to each other. Every part of the relationship then blossoms and becomes fruitful. Problems which once brought division will be used to bring husband and wife closer together. The physical relation-

ship in marriage becomes completely fulfilling---once other
basic needs are met.

When a husband and wife recognize each other's needs, a
life-long commitment to satisfy those longings can and
should be made.

RESOLVE DIFFERENCES GOD'S WAY

God's Word forbids divorce and remarriage. In the
Sermon on the Mount, the Lord Jesus said:

> It hath been said, Whosoever shall put away his wife, let him
> give her a writing of divorcement: But I say unto you, That
> whosoever shall put away his wife, saving for the cause of
> fornication causeth her to commit adultery: and whosoever
> shall marry her that is divorced committeth adultery (Matthew
> 5:31-32).

Long before a man or a woman "puts away" his or her
partner in divorce, there is always a "putting away" of the
person from real companionship, communication, and
oneness. When the real closeness and union in a marriage
is broken, the partners are forced into a subtle form of
adultery. They seek to have their needs for companionship,
meaningful conversation, oneness, attention, and respect
fulfilled by someone other than their marriage partners.
This is "adultery." Adultery has a broader meaning than
just illicit sexual union outside marriage. God described
Israel's worship of false gods and seeking help from them
as "adultery." *Adultery, in a broad sense, can be understood as seeking to have needs met and fulfilled other than
through the God-ordained channel and method.* Therefore
if a man "puts away" his wife from real oneness with
himself and she seeks a substitute in soap operas, books,
materialism, a job, or other things he has forced her into a
form of adultery. This type of "adultery" always precedes
the actual illicit physical union outside marriage.

Such "putting away,"---the breaking of real oneness and
communication in marriage---results from unresolved differences, unhealed hurts and unforgiven offenses. Often
the differences are very small. If they are not resolved,
however, they will destroy real communication and oneness
in marriage. The couple may continue sharing a house,

smiling at one another, and having a physical relationship (although it will not really satisfy). However, the real union is ended.

Because some hurt has not been healed, one partner "puts away" the other from the very center of his life and existence. The "putting away" may be done when the expectations of one partner are dashed again and again. To avoid further hurts, the offended partner withdraws and erects a wall of protection to keep from being hurt again. The hurt person may also seek to "get even." This hurts, offends, or irritates the other party. He or she then erects a barrier or wall also. Even if divorce does not result (and it does not in many, many situations) the marriage relationship becomes a stiff, cold, formal one without real life and love and meaningful communication. The partners no longer meet one another's needs. "Adultery" (physical or emotional) results as empty people seek fulfillment outside marriage.

God recognized the danger. It can happen in marriage or in any relationship between people. In two places in the Gospel of Matthew, the Lord Jesus gives procedures and assigns responsibilities through which all wrongs and hurts can be healed. In Matthew 18:15 the Lord says:

> Moreover if thy brother shall trespass against thee, go and tell him his fault between thee and him alone: if he shall hear thee, thou hast gained thy brother.

Going to the person who has offended *with a proper attitude* is the key to seeing the difference resolved. No matter what someone else has done, we have no right to get angry, irritated, or upset. The proper way to approach a person who has offended is to go quietly and say, "I need to ask your forgiveness. I got very upset with you because of _____. It was wrong for me to react this way. Will you forgive me?" In ninety-nine cases out of one-hundred the other person will grant forgiveness and also seek forgiveness for his or her own wrongdoing. The offender may or may not acknowledge his own wrongdoing immediately. Therefore, give the Lord time to work on him, once you have confessed your own wrong attitudes or reactions.

Taking the blame in this way without looking at the wrongs of the other party is God's way of reconciliation.

The Lord Jesus, in seeking to restore fellowship between God and man, took upon Himself everything which separated us from God. He took all of man's sin and shame and guilt. Once He took our sin, we were made free to come back to Him. Our union with Him was renewed. He is to be our pattern. In Ephesians 4:32 we are told to forgive one another as He forgives us. The Bible says:

> And be ye kind one to another, tenderhearted, forgiving one another, even as God for Christ's sake hath forgiven you.

How did the Lord forgive?

Christ has done no wrong. Yet he took all of our guilt and blame and shame and punishment. For this reason we were freed to be one with Him again. We should be willing to do the same for others—and particularly for our marriage partner. When we truly forgive, we must put ourselves in the place where we can be hurt again. This is what the Lord Jesus commanded in the Sermon on the Mount. He said that instead of getting even (an eye for an eye and a tooth for a tooth) we should turn the other cheek (expose ourselves to getting hurt again).

We have the same obligation when we realize that someone (including our husband or wife) feels wronged by us.

God says that if we realize (or sense) that we have offended someone we should go and get it settled. The surest way to settle any difference is by using God's way of reconciliation. If we ask God, He will show us our fault.

Once forgiveness is granted, the foundation is laid for restoring communication and an openness in marriage. Without it, little differences and hurts erect high walls between two people who are supposed to be one. In effect, one or both partners "puts away" the other. Even if no divorce results (immediately or longterm), one of two things happen. The home may become an "armed camp" or where there are few open battles, the relationship becomes a distant, formal one without the real oneness and blessings which marriage should produce.

To avoid this tragedy, marriage partners should really commit themselves to resolving differences God's way, rather than just "getting over them."

TRUST ONE ANOTHER

A stable, secure marriage has to be built on mutual trust. There must be trust to forgive. There must be trust to go on when the other person has failed. The alternative to trust is jealousy, suspicion, or protective walls built to hide behind. We can give unconditional trust to our partner only if we trust the Lord to keep him right—or straighten him out when he fails. Husbands and wives must commit themselves to earning the trust of their partners. This trust is commanded and demanded by the Word of God. Of woman, the Bible says:

> Who can find a virtuous woman? for her price is far above rubies. The heart of her husband doth safely *trust* in her. . . (Proverbs 31:10-11a).

Wives need to trust their husbands also. Only by trusting can a woman obey the Word of God which says:

> Wives, submit yourselves unto your own husbands, as unto the Lord. (Ephesians 5:22).

Trusting God or our partner cannot be based on feeling or what is likely to happen. Trust is the result of a decision which we act upon.

SUMMARY

Accepting and consistently applying these seven basic prerequisites will build stable, secure homes. Husbands and wives should study and memorize the foundational concepts for a stable marriage. Whenever one partner or the other senses that differences are developing in the home, prayerfully checking the list will show the cause. By faithfully following this practice, either partner in the marriage can be used of God to build a stable, secure home which cannot be destroyed.

Chapter XII

A MARRIAGE
THAT SATISFIES

> *And God said, Let us make man in our image, after our*
> *likeness: and let them have dominion over the fish of the*
> *sea, and over the fowl of the air, and over the cattle, and*
> *over all the earth, and over every creeping thing that*
> *creepeth upon the earth. So God created man in his own*
> *image, in the image of God created he him; male and female*
> *created he them.*
>
> ---*Genesis 1:26-27*

TO BE COMPLETELY HAPPY, a marriage needs more than stability. For true blessedness a husband and wife must be finding complete satisfaction and fulfillment in the marriage. To achieve this, each partner must understand and accept his particular God-given role in the home and be working to fulfill it.

Men and women are to have different roles in marriage and the home. This is shown in the way they are made. God made men and women differently. They were created different physically. They are different in how they react emotionally. Men and women look at and evaluate things from different perspectives. This did not just happen or "evolve." It was carefully planned in the mind of God. The differences God builds into men and women equip each partner in a marriage uniquely to fulfill his or her God-given role. True blessedness in life can only be achieved when God's plan is being fulfilled.

The first step toward building a marriage that satisfies is to recognize the roles God gives to each partner. Let's look at what God wants from each partner in a marriage.

RECOGNIZE GOD-GIVEN ROLES

God has planned for fathers to be everything to their families that He, our Heavenly Father, is to us. That is why the husband, the head of the family, is called "father." The wife, by the same token, is to be everything to her husband that the church (His bride) is to Christ. By carefully studying the relationship of Christ to the church, husbands and wives can learn the roles God has planned for them.

To understand a father's many responsibilities, look at our Heavenly Father's relationship to us. According to the Lord's prayer, God the Father. . .

. . .is over everything (Our Father which art *in heaven*). So too, earthly fathers are to be the heads of their families. (See Ephesians 5:23)

. . .God the Father is to be respected (Hallowed be thy name). Earthly fathers are to be reverenced by their wives and children. (See Ephesians 5:33-6:3)

. . .God the Father is to rule. He is to be obeyed immediately, completely and cheerfully (Thy kingdom come, Thy will be done on earth, as it is in heaven). The husband and father is to rule his house well (See I Timothy 3:12) which requires that he be obeyed immediately, completely, and cheerfully.

. . .Our Heavenly Father is our Provider (Give us this day our daily bread). So too, the earthly father is the primary provider for his wife and children. (See I Timothy 5:8)

. . .by understanding the true significance and results of praying "Forgive us our debts as we forgive our debtors" we see that we are asking our Heavenly Father to oversee and enforce right relationships between us and others. So too, an earthly father is responsible for developing and enforcing harmonious and scriptural relationships between members of his family (See I Timothy 3:5). Family members should expect him to do so.

. . .our Heavenly Father leads and guides us morally (lead us not into temptation). An earthly father gives his family this leadership and protection as he teaches them the right way to go. (See Ephesians 5:25-28 and Ephesians 6:4)

. . .we need our Heavenly Father to protect and safeguard us from evil (deliver us from evil). So, too, earthly fathers must safeguard their families from false religious doctrines, materialism, humanism, worldly and ungodly amusements,

TV, and literature, while providing wholesome alternatives.
The father should be looked to and appreciated for his
providing this protection.

Being a father is awesome. The man is to be as responsible for his family in all of these areas as the Heavenly
Father is. Children get their earliest and most important
ideas about God from their earthly fathers. When fathers
do a poor job, their children may grow up thinking God is
like their earthly fathers---impatient, self-centered, ill-
tempered, unfaithful to keep promises, unavailable, or
unloving.

Unless a father accepts his God-given responsibilities
and actively works toward fulfilling them, he cannot be
truly satisfied in life. No matter what he may achieve on the
job, in church, or the community, his life will be empty if he
is not fulfilling God's plan for his home. To combat often
unrecognizable emptiness and frustration, the father must
fulfill his God-given responsibilities by deciding to serve
the Lord as Joshua did. As Israel settled in the promised
land, Joshua said:

> And if it seem evil unto you to serve the Lord, choose you this
> day whom you will serve; whether the gods which your fathers
> served that were on the other side of the flood, or the gods of the
> Amorites, in whose land ye dwell; *but as for me and my house
> we will serve the Lord* (Joshua 24:15).

Having made this decision, a father must teach and lead
his family in serving the Lord. He must be sensitive to
spiritual needs of each family member and their relationship with others. He must love his wife and children as the
Lord Jesus loved the church and gave Himself for it. No
matter how much a father does or provides, if he does not
love, he is nothing. The Bible warns in I Corinthians 13:1:

> Though I speak with the tongues of men and of angels, and
> have not love I am become as sounding brass, or a tinkling
> cymbal.

In attempting to be everything to his wife and family that
the Heavenly Father is to us, a husband needs help in an
infinite number of ways. God made woman to be "an help
meet" for the man (Genesis 2:18).

As this "help meet," a woman is to be to her husband

what the church (Christ's bride) is intended to be to the Lord Jesus. A survey of the scripture shows how big and exciting that job is. The Bible teaches that the church is to. . .

. . .allow God to fulfill His nature as a giver and provider by being totally dependent upon Him for every need. Likewise, a wife allows her husband to fulfill his role as a provider, protector, lover, etc. by being totally dependent upon him. In doing so, she "completes" her husband.

. . .the church works out and carries out the details needed to fulfill the goals, plans and purposes of the Lord Jesus for the world. Likewise, a wife as an "help meet" supplies the vitally important details that make a husband's dreams and plans for his family become reality.

. . .as the "salt of the earth," the church makes the world a safer, cleaner, more orderly, more pleasant place to live. A wife applies her time, talent, ingenuity, resourcefulness, love, and femininity to make her family's home a refuge from the world's trials, troubles, tribulation, and turmoil. By making her home what God intends, a wife and mother gives her family a little taste of "heaven on earth."

. . .by witnessing and preaching the Word, the church helps people become God's spiritual "babies." It is then responsible for training them to be mature, responsible Christians. Just as the Lord is totally dependent on the church to bear and train His spiritual children, so too, a husband can experience the joy of fatherhood only as his wife brings their children into the world and supplies the minute-by-minute training to develop godly character in them.

The church is to respond to Christ's love and provision with obedience, reverence, thanksgiving and fellowship, giving praise to all men for all He does and to Him for all that He is. A wife "completes" her husband and is totally satisfied herself when she has this same relationship with her husband.

When she recognizes how important the church is to the Lord Jesus, the woman can visualize the important, exciting job God has given her to fulfill at her husband's side.

Just as a husband cannot be satisfied unless he is fulfilling the role God has for him, the woman also will be empty and frustrated if she is not fulfilling the work God has given her to do.

Like Christ and His bride, wives and husbands are to live together, maintaining oneness and fellowship. The husband is the head. He sets the goals and makes long-range plans. His wife implements the details. This is a true "help meet."

Even though her husband is to be her head and her provider, a wife is not to be a docile slave. She is *to share* in her husband's dreams and goals. She has the same right of "appeal" that the church has to Jesus Christ. When a wife "delights herself in her husband" and her other attitudes and appeals duplicate the conditions which the Lord Jesus gave the church for answered prayer, she will find that her husband, like the Lord, will say:

If you ask anything, I will do it. (See John 14:13-14.)

In fulfilling her God-given role, a wife needs wisdom to develop methods and to work out details to keep her family functioning smoothly if her God-given responsibility is to be fulfilled. Through many crises, she must trust God to make her a loving mother, nutrition expert, chauffeur, a seamstress, nurse, teacher, wise counselor, purchasing wizard, referee, and mediator. Through it all she must be kind, loving, and understanding. Like the church, she must take her husband's dreams and instructions and provide the details which produce liveable reality.

Most of all, she needs to learn to recognize his love and respond to it. Wives must learn to. . .

. . .be sober, to love their husbands, to love their children, To be discreet, chaste, keepers at home, good, obedient to their husbands, that the word of God be not blasphemed (Titus 2:4-5).

Truly, the roles of men and women in the marriage relationship are to be different.

MADE DIFFERENT

Because their roles are different, God made men and women to be different. For example, because food has to be produced "by the sweat of the face" (Genesis 3:19), man was made physically stronger than woman. His greater physical strength equips him for two things: doing hard labor and protecting his home and family.

Man is to be the head of the home and provide overall

leadership and guidance. Therefore, God made men with minds which tend to see long-range general needs, goals, threats, and problems. Woman, made to be a help meet, tends to see and be concerned about details.

Conflicts and great frustration can result in the home when men look only at the overall picture and women look only at the details. That's why they must learn that they were made different in order to complement one another. A man looks at his house. He dreams of home improvement projects that he would like to complete during the next four years. His wife, meanwhile, is more concerned about having the dripping faucet in the bathroom fixed *now*. While the husband thinks about adding a garbage disposal next fall, his wife worries about the garbage that needs to be taken out *tonight*. The husband thinks and plans toward financing a college education for his ten-year-old son. His wife is more concerned about where the money will come from to buy the boy new shoes *this Friday*.

Differences like these can cause real friction in a marriage. To keep bitterness from developing, marriage partners need to recognize and understand that they are made to look at things differently.

Exactly the same kind of problems can develop between us and God. God is planning for eternity. He is working to make us like the Lord Jesus Christ. That is His long-range goal. In accomplishing His purpose, God often uses events that hurt. God uses painful experiences to chip away qualities in our character that are not Christ-like. When we experience these difficult times, we can get bitter at God. All we see are the unpleasant details that hurt. We want God to fix them *right now,* but He is working toward the long-range goal. If we become impatient or bitter toward Him, our fellowship is marred. Our joy and peace vanish. We are miserable until by faith we can say, "Thank You, Lord. I don't know what You are doing but You do. I know that You will bring good out of it."

Long-range goals and short-term needs are both important in the home. They are also important in our relationship with the Lord. Unless both marriage partners see that their differing interests, goals, needs, and insights complement one another, real frustration and conflicts will develop. Both partners in a marriage need to realize that God made them functionally one. They need to see how their differences fit together to make a beautiful whole. In this way, a husband and wife can grow in appreciation for one another and for the God who planned it all.

DIFFERENCES NEED TO BE MAINTAINED

God intends for these differences that He has built into men and women to be recognized, maintained and appreciated. He has devised safeguards to keep the differences from being ignored, forgotten, eroded or erased. For example, He forbids women to wear men's clothing and men to wear women's garments. He says:

> The woman shall not wear that which pertaineth unto a man, neither shall a man put on a woman's garment: for all that do so are abomination unto the Lord thy God. (Deuteronomy 22:5)

Men and women are also to be recognized as different by the length of their hair. They are to maintain this difference. The Bible says:

> Doth not even nature itself teach you, that, if a man have long hair, it is a shame unto him? But if a woman have long hair, it is a glory to her: for her hair is given her for a covering. (I Corinthians 11:14-15)

These differences which God has erected as safeguards are being brushed aside or ignored. It has become accepted in our culture for women to wear masculine-type trousers, shirts, ties, suits and short hair styles. Many men are wearing long hair with effeminate styling. Some are even wearing effeminate fur coats, earrings, necklaces, and carry feminine-type purses. Those who do so say by their actions that God didn't know what He was doing when He made the sexes different. Homosexuals, by their perverted pairing off, say the same thing. God applies the same label to homosexual activity, long hair on men, and the wearing of men's clothes by women and vice versa. All are abomination to God. All these attempts to erase or eliminate the precious differences which God made between men and women are abomination to Him.

Differences between the sexes are shown in many ways in the Bible. One final example is in the instruction God gives to men and women about dress and conduct. In I

Timothy 2:9 God says:

> In like manner also, [I will] that women adorn themselves in modest apparel.

While women are told to be modest, men are not. He has different instructions for men and women concerning dress because they are different sexually. Men are stirred sexually by what they see. That is why women are told to dress modestly. Women are different. Women react to a man's touch or caress. This is why God tells women to be modest but tells men:

> Now concerning the things whereof ye wrote unto me: It is good for a man not to touch a woman (I Corinthians 7:1).

When men and women are careful to obey God's Word, neither will unfairly stir desires within the opposite sex which can only be legitimately fulfilled in marriage.

As these differences between the sexes have been eroded in recent years, further problems have developed. Men are taking on more and more feminine characteristics, and are also wearing fewer clothes. Girls and women, at the same time, have become the aggressors in "touching" men.

Outward distinctions designed by God to demonstrate the differences between men and women have been almost totally eliminated in today's society. As outward differences are being blurred, the distinctive roles which men and women are supposed to have in the home and marriage are being destroyed as well.

Today, 60% of all mothers are gainfully employed. Almost half the mothers with preschool children work outside the home. Fathers are no longer the primary providers for their families. Mothers with full-time jobs outside the home have difficulty providing their families with homes which are "a little bit of Heaven on earth."

When a man is not the primary provider for the family and the woman is not primarily a "help meet" and "keeper at home," both are in conflict with God's scheme of things. There will be dissatisfaction, emptiness and lack of fulfillment in their lives. Frustration and emptiness will result from not doing and being what God intended. To be fully satisfied, both husbands and wives need only to be fulfilling their own God-given roles. A wife will feel cheated and somehow incomplete (although she may not know why) if her husband is not truly her provider, protector, and spiritual head. A husband will feel cheated and incomplete (although he may not know why) if his wife is not a real "help meet" who provides him with a home which is "a little bit of Heaven on earth."*

For 6000 years men and women generally accepted and fulfilled God-given roles. As a result families were basically stable and happy. As recently as 1900 only one marriage in one-hundred failed. Today it is one out of two.

Skyrocketing divorce rates are not caused by mounting financial pressures, marrying too young, immaturity, promiscuous sex standards before or during marriage, "incompatability," drugs and alcohol, or being too involved in jobs and careers. Even the "women's rights movement" is not the cause. These are all just symptoms of deeper troubles.

The symptoms develop when a marriage is not satisfying. Sadly, most Americans are suffering from a lack of satisfaction in marriage. Many husbands and wives feel that somehow they are missing "something." Often they do not know why they are dissatisfied. They just sense an emptiness. To fill that hunger, many seek satisfaction in "things." Cars, clothing, children, a redecorated or larger home, and vacations are all looked to for fulfillment.

Such substitutes do not provide a satisfaction that lasts. They do not fill the real need. They are like drinking water or chewing gum to cover hunger pangs when dieting. Water and gum do not satisfy for long. Neither are "things" and activities an adequate substitute for the true satisfaction which can be found only by fulfilling God-given roles in marriage. The substitutes cannot satisfy and they are costly. The financial problems of many families result from seeking satisfactions in "things."

As financial pressures mount, many seek the next escape

----

*Wives should never work outside the home until children start to school. Even then, great precautions are needed. If a wife senses that her role as the provider of a home which is a "little bit of heaven on earth" is suffering, she should not work or should modify the work schedule. Realizing that she is getting more satisfaction or fulfillment from her job than from being a wife and mother is another danger sign.

in alcohol, drugs, affairs and sex outside marriage. Frequently, divorce is the final escape. But then the tragic pattern starts all over.

Tragically, many husbands and wives never fulfill their God-given roles in marriage because they have never actually been taught what they are. Since World War II most "main-line" church denominations have moved away from the Bible. Having done so, they have no basis for teaching God's way to build Bible-based homes.

Churches which have remained faithful to the Bible have often failed also. They have allowed a needed emphasis on teaching and defending the Bible and the fundamental doctrines of the faith to detract from also teaching God's order for the home.

What is the remedy? Now that you have been given the foundational truths on which to build a good marriage, purpose in your heart to fulfill your God-given role. By doing so, you will start experiencing the satisfaction God gives when we do what we should. As you fulfill your role in the home, God will make you a blessing to your husband or wife. This will create a desire in your mate to be a full-fledged marriage partner as well.

A SOLVENT HOME IS A HAPPY HOME

Take no thought for your life, what ye shall eat, or what ye shall drink; nor yet for your body, what ye shall put on . . . . But seek ye first the kingdom of God and his righteousness; and all these things shall be added unto you.

---Matthew 6:25, 33

SQUABBLES OVER MONEY are often blamed for the breakup of the family. Tensions caused by financial problems can strain even good marriages. Money problems have two basic causes. Some result from poor financial training and example while growing up. Others are symptoms of deep-rooted spiritual and emotional needs.

Families who lack security and real satisfaction in marriage frequently try to fill the emptiness with "things." Unbalanced budgets, mounting debts, and makeshift rescue-attempts result. This increases pressures on already strained marriage relationships. When the breakup comes, finances are blamed.

There is no easy way to achieve financial freedom. It can be done, however. It can be accomplished only as marriage partners work to establish a stable, secure, satisfying relationship.

When the principles for a stable, satisfying home and marriage are recognized and accepted, a family can start working to get tangled finances in order. Many troubled families have found financial freedom through a comprehensive eight-point program. At first glance, the steps may seem illogical. They work, however, because they are based on God's unchanging principles. The eight point program includes:

> START TITHING: Give the first tenth of all income to the Lord as the Bible commands. As illogical as it seems, it works. God says, "Give and it shall be given unto you" (Luke 6:38).

> STOP all credit buying. Cut up all credit cards and cancel charge accounts.

> ELIMINATE ALL DEBT as quickly as possible (even if it takes years). Then stay out of debt no matter what emergencies arise.

> CUT EXPENSES. Eliminate luxuries and non-essentials. Wise buying of essentials and eliminating waste can save many families up to 20% of their total income.

> EVALUATE whether a working mother can contribute as much or more to *actual* family income by staying home and doing part-time typing, babysitting of one or two children, etc.

> SEEK to be like the Lord Jesus and give Him control of your life. God promises in Matthew 6:33 that He will provide all of our material needs if we will accept His goals for our lives.

> TELL OTHERS what you are trusting God to do. Psalm 31:19 says that God has great things stored up for those who trust in Him and that He works them out for those who trust in Him *before others*.

> START A SYSTEMATIC SAVINGS PROGRAM for future purchases of things now bought on credit, children's education, vacations, and eventual retirement.

Thousands of families have seen God work real miracles once a firm commitment is made to put all finances on a Scriptural basis. Some of the steps seem illogical or impossible. However, faith in God must be based on His promises rather than on what seems logically possible or probable. Prayerfully study these eight steps and the Scriptural basis for them.

TITHE

As illogical as it may seem, the first step toward financial freedom is to start giving. God makes tremendous promises to those who give. The promise, "Give, and it shall be given unto you," has already been examined. In Malachi 3:8-12, God says:

> Will a man rob God? Yet ye have robbed me. But ye say,

> Wherein have we robbed thee? In tithes and offerings.
>
> Ye are cursed with a curse: for ye have robbed me, even this whole nation. Bring ye all the tithes into the storehouse, that there be meat in mine house, and prove me now herewith, saith the Lord of hosts, if I will not open you the windows of heaven, and pour you out a blessing, that there shall not be room enough to receive it.
>
> And I will rebuke the devourer for your sakes, and he shall not destroy the fruits of your ground; neither shall your vine cast her fruit before the time in the field, saith the Lord of hosts. And all nations shall call you blessed: for ye shall be a delightsome land, saith the Lord of hosts.

Analyze these verses carefully. They show that by failing to tithe, a person (1) robs God, (2) is under a curse, (3) keeps God from proving His ability to provide, (4) keeps the windows of blessing closed (5) opens himself to the attacks of the devourer (Satan), (6) exposes his vines and fields (that which produces his income) to Satanic destruction, and (7) misses the opportunity to be blessed and be recognized as blessed.

Two ladies heard a message on tithing. One said "How I wish we could tithe---but we've never been able to afford it." Her friend, whose family income was much less, said, "We figure we can't afford not to tithe." The second lady and her husband had learned that trusting and obeying God is the only pathway to blessing.

A simple story from America's history illustrates this truth. About sixty years ago a history teacher at the Manual Training High School in Denver named Rhodes recalled for his students how at age four he had traveled across the Great Plains in an oxcart driven by his father. This is the story he told to his students:

> The wagon train set out from St. Joseph, Missouri heading for Denver on a Monday morning late in the spring in the early 1860's. Things went well for the first week. The wagon train covered a lot of territory. Day by day they moved across the open plains and rolling hills of Kansas. Each night as they camped, the wagons were drawn into a circle. It was Indian territory.
>
> Early the first Sunday morning Mr. Rhodes's father faced a situation he had not expected. The other men began to break

camp, obviously intending to travel. Elder Rhodes, being a man of God and of conviction, protested the plan to travel on God's day. His appeal was not heeded. The other men said, "We're travelling. You can do as you please. Remain here if you want to—and became Indian bait." When Elder Rhodes showed that he would not travel on God's day, two other families decided to stand with him. They remained in camp, studied the Bible and rested while the main train moved westward over the rolling hills and out of sight.

Monday morning the three families journeyed on by themselves. Thus it was through the second week. However, by Saturday night they caught up with the main group and pulled into camp. We can imagine that as they came into sight some of the unbelieving ones probably said, "Here come those fools driving hard to catch up with us to be under our protection. You can bet they've learned their lesson."

Did those three families feel any safer that Saturday night than they had the six previous ones? Not a bit. The next morning, being Sunday, again the main group broke camp and traveled on as usual, but the three families rested and worshiped the Lord. By the following Thursday evening they overtook the main group once more. The unbelievers said anew, "Look at this. Here come those racing fools again."

By this time the main camp should have learned the benefits of rest and the benefits of doing things God's way. But it happened to them as Isaiah said:

Let favour be shewed to the wicked, yet will he not learn righteousness (. . . . for he is) ever learning, and never able to come to the knowledge of the truth. (Isaiah 26:10, II Timothy 3:7)

Friday morning the three families were away first. They had faith to believe that the God who protected them when they were behind the main group could care for them out ahead of the others. As they stopped each evening, they claimed the promise of God's Word which says:

The angel of the Lord encampeth round about them that fear him, and delivereth them (Psalm 34:7).

Sunday they rested again, and Sunday evening the main group moved in slowly and spent the evening with them. Monday morning was no "Blue Monday" for Elder Rhodes and his small company---but it was for the cursing main camp. The three families were off first again. They never saw the main group on the plains after the third Sunday. Here's how the story ended:

> The three families arrived in Denver two weeks ahead of those who left St. Joseph with them. They were in the finest spirit and health, rejoicing as Ezra did that "God's good hand was upon them" (Ezra 7:9). Their oxen and equipment were in the best of shape and brought the fanciest of prices on the Denver market. Good outfits were in great demand. Two weeks later when the rest came dragging in, they were sick, cursing and irritable. Their equipment was broken down and their oxen worn out.

The faith and obedience of Elder Rhodes was passed down to his son. In the years before his retirement as a teacher, he would tell the story and show his New Testament which was ever with him at his desk. His students learned an important lesson from life about the wisdom of knowing God's Word and obeying it---even when it did not seem logical. One of those students, Carl R. Steelburg, put the story on paper so that we can profit from it today.

Resting one day out of seven, particularly if you are in a hurry or have a long way to go, is not logical. However, this true story from America's history demonstrates that "trusting and obeying" God is the only "smart" way to live. The same conclusion applies to tithing. The first step toward getting out of debt and finding financial freedom is to start giving God the first tenth of all income.

Many people know that the Bible teaches that everyone should tithe. They say, "We'll do it just as soon as we get our finances in order." They are never able to start tithing, however. They are just like the seven day travelers who fell far behind those who traveled for six days and rested on the seventh. The first step toward getting family finances in order is to start tithing by faith.

STOP ALL CREDIT BUYING

"Easy" credit has been a way of life in America for several generations. Each generation has gone a little deeper into debt. As a result, many young people have never had the training or the example needed to establish a sound financial basis for marriage. Often they start marriage in debt from the rings, the wedding, the honeymoon, etc.* Many young marrieds immediately want all the things their parents worked years to get. Then they borrow for furniture, appliances, a car, and other items. Soon they find themselves in bondage to the lenders.

If the marriage is not growing in stability and satisfaction, these initial problems will multiply. Financial woes will deepen as security and satisfaction are sought in "things" and activities which cost money. Some seller or lender will always be willing to extend credit—or increase credit limits.

Life becomes an endless treadmill of running feverishly but never quite catching up with all the payments. The family never knows the freedom and joy of being able to decide how to use current income to satisfy a current want or desire. Every paycheck (and lots of future ones) is committed to paying off debts for clothes which no longer fit, cars which are no longer new, vacations which are long past, and other purchases which no longer satisfy.

Going into debt for day-to-day needs and wants (food, clothing, cars, maintenance, furniture, appliances, TV's, stereos, remodeling, vacations, and unexpected sickness) violates God's Word. The Bible says:

> Owe no man anything, but to love one another (Romans 13:8).

Whenever a Bible command like this one is violated, suffering follows. Proverbs 22:7 tells the consequences of debt. The Bible says:

> ... the borrower is servant to the lender.

. A personal case history might be helpful at this point. Long before I ever learned that God said, "Owe no man anything," I learned the hard way that credit buying and debts enslave. I learned that the borrower is, as the Bible says, "servant to the lender." Here's the story:

I learned about the joys of living on credit when I was 19 years old—and the perils of it a few weeks later. I had a good job as a manager of a radio station branch office in a county

----

*Young couples should postpone marriage until they are completely out of debt. A joint commitment should be made before marriage to a firm "pay-as-we-go" policy.

seat in Pennsylvania ($40 a week was good money in 1948).
One week I was a little short on cash and the owner of the
restaurant in which I usually ate offered to let me sign the
check. He extended the same privilege to other regular
customers.

It was great. I ate all week---and had the cash I usually
spent for food to spend for other things. When payday came
I settled the bill and then found I had no real choice of
where to eat that week. Because my meal money had
already been spent to settle last week's account, I ate at
Bill's throughout the following week. This went on for
several weeks until I discovered that the gas station where I
bought gas for my car would also let me sign the tickets and
settle up on payday.

Again I was free---for a while. I did not overdo it, but I
broke the monotony of eating at Bill's by visiting another
restaurant for a nice steak. I also visited a neighboring
town for a shrimp feed.

It took only a few weeks of financing the extras I wanted
by buying gasoline on credit to get me in a complete bind
there also. I lived with the consequences for a while. Then I
learned that my landlady whom I usually paid in advance
was willing to wait until the end of the week for the room
rent. I was free to enjoy life, but again not for long.

It took only several months of spending money that I did
not have for things I did not need to put me into total
bondage. I maintained a good credit rating by paying each
week's debt to the restaurant owner, the gas station
operator and my landlady. Then each week I would start
the whole vicious cycle over. I was no longer free to decide
how and when and where I would spend my paycheck. It
was all committed by the time I got it. It ws a miserable way
to live!

> Even then I did not learn. Because I had a good credit rating, I
> found that the restaurant owner would take a partial payment
> on the previous week's meals. That gave me a little extra money
> to spend the way I wanted to---for one week---but then I was
> deeper in debt. Soon I was a number of weeks behind at the
> restaurant, the gas station, and with my landlady.

When I was offered a better job at another radio station

fifty miles away, I could not leave town until I borrowed money from my father to pay my bills. In the new city to which I moved I did not have a credit rating; and I was very careful not to establish one. Months of frugal living enabled me to pay my dad the money I had borrowed. My parents tried to teach me the concept of "owe no man anything," but I had to learn the hard way.

I made the rule then and have followed it since—if I can not pay for it with cash, I do not buy it. It was a painful but valuable lesson. Fortunately, the girl I married also had parents who believed "owe no man anything." This principle has been followed consistently throughout our marriage.

Over the years we have saved thousands and thousands of dollars in interest charges. I have saved much more in another way. I have found that sometimes the thing I am sure I want and need does not seem nearly so necessary if I can pay for it right then. I then hold onto the cash for something I really need or want. Best of all, we have enjoyed freedom throughout our married life from the awful bondage that debt brings.

ELIMINATE ALL DEBT

Living on the credit treadmill puts tremendous pressure on a marriage. Children feel the tension also. The family never gets to enjoy all of the things it could have bought with the thousands of dollars spent over the years for interest and carrying charges. The family which uses credit suffers spiritual loss also. Family members miss the joy of seeing God provide in miraculous ways in answer to prayer.

Even though a family stops credit buying, it may take years to eliminate debts. (Most experts consider that "consumer" debt for depreciating items such as furniture, clothes, TV's, appliances, cars, etc. is different from a mortgage on real property such as a home which can be expected to retain or increase its value.) Real belt tightening may be necessary. It will take careful planning to pay cash for absolute necessities while paying off old installment debts, but it can be done. Each of the seven steps to financial freedom must be implemented.

Christians who have committed themselves to "eliminating all debt" can give exciting testimonies of how God has worked to get them out of debt long before they thought it possible.

CUT EXPENSES

Important financial decisions such as determining to starting tithing and cease credit buying need to be made once and then followed faithfully---even in times of emergency. Controlling family expenses, however, requires continual lifelong effort. Cutting expenses will pay big dividends. Many families can cut monthly expenditures by 10/25%. That sounds amazing but it is possible. Here are ways others have made sizable savings:

> Completely eliminate cigarettes, beer, soft drinks, packaged snacks, junk foods, and candy from the family diet and budget. Nutrition will be aided and health will be improved and many families can save $100 to $250 a month in the family "food" budget.

In addition to the financial savings, families might be amazed at the improved behavior and attitude of their children. Dr. Lendon Smith, the author of *Improving Your Child's Behavior Chemistry,* and other child-care experts have seen remarkable changes in the behavior of even seriously-disturbed children when junk foods are eliminated from the diet. The experience of a Christian summer camp youth ministry in Manitou Springs, Colorado confirms Dr. Smith's findings. A few years ago when candy and soft drink machines were replaced by a machine which dispenses only canned fruit juice, a remarkable change was seen immediately. The nightly battles to get young people settled down to sleep ended with the banning of snacks containing refined sugar, chemical additives, and caffeine.

Law enforcement officials have made similar discoveries. The president of the International Juvenile Officers Association, Lt. Frank Schaefer, says widespread consumption of junk foods by teen-agers may be a factor in growing juvenile crime rates. Testifying that he has witnessed drastic behaviorial changes in twelve and thirteen year olds, the 33-year police veteran said:

> They lose control of themselves and nearly go out of their minds. Junk foods, especially soda, are harmful to kids . . . .the

sugar is not good for them.

Disciplinary problems fell 48% at the Tidewater, Virgina detention center when sugar in the diet of 276 juvenile inmates was drastically reduced as a test. Delinquents who developed consistently good behaviour rose by 71% at the same time. Soft drinks and junk food snacks were replaced with fruit juices, fruits and nuts and sweetened cereals were eliminated from the diet. Honey and molasses were substituted for refined sugar in cooking.

Once unnecessary "foods" are eliminated, care in buying and preparing of essentials can produce additional savings. Here's how:

> Plan menus to use meats, produce, etc. which are on "special." In many metropolitan areas during 1980-83, for example, frying chickens varied in price during any one month period from .39¢ a pound to .69¢, depending on whether they were on special. During the month, prices on chuck roasts ranged from $1.09 to $1.89 a pound. A wise shopper buys all the chickens or chuck roasts, etc. the family will use during the month when they are on special. Savings of 40% to 60% can be realized.

> Watch for similar extra-special prices on regularly-used staple items such as canned goods, rice, beans, spaghetti, and other such food items and cleaning supplies, toilet tissue, toothpaste, soap, light bulbs, etc. Buy three-or-six-month supplies. Savings of 25% to 40% or more can be realized---totaling hundreds of dollars a year.

Using day-old bakery goods and reduced-price meats and produce can also make sizable savings possible. For example:

> At least two St. Louis area supermarket chains feature "jet-fresh" fish and seafood. The fish arrives in the stores on Wednesday or Thursday. Packages are marked for sale through the following Tuesday. The fresh seafood is expensive. However, what is still in stock is often available at half price by Monday afternoon or Tuesday morning. Cooked and eaten Tuesday evenings, the family can enjoy delicacies at a fraction of full cost.

Wise housewives watch for similar bargains in fresh produce. For example:

> One lady is a regular customer in several markets for "too ripe to sell" fruits and vegetables. When bargains are available, she

"drops everything" in her regular schedule, buys large quantities, and cans or freezes them for later use. Purchases can sometimes be made for one-tenth or one-fifth of the regular price. The quality is excellent if used, canned, or frozen immediately.

Other ways of cutting family expenses include:

Plan to cook meals from "scratch." Avoid higher cost frozen, ready to warm, convenience foods, TV dinners, etc.

Figure unit costs on all purchases and buy the most economical sizes (the larger-size package may or may not be the most economical). Some super markets post the cost per ounce on the shelves. Others do not. Some careful shoppers figure unit prices with a pocket calculator.

By carefully clipping and systematically filing coupons from the food sections of newspapers, considerable savings can be realized. Even greater savings can be enjoyed by holding the coupons until the items covered are offered at extra-special prices by the store. Care must be taken to resist buying luxury and convenience items just because a coupon is available. Develop the discipline to clip and save coupons only for needed items.

Eating at home saves money. It also provides a time for family fellowship. There is not much fellowship in the line at Wendy's, guzzling Big Mac's, or eating pizza while rock music blares in the background. Meal time at home can be a vitally important time for drawing the family together.

Refrain from window shopping. Avoid impulse buying. All purchases of needed items should be carefully planned. Clothing, for example, can be bought for next year at end-of-the season sales. Tremendous savings can sometimes be realized.

All sorts of needed items can be found at garage sales, flea markets and the growing number of stores which sell used (but practically new) things on consignment for the owners.

Utility costs can be reduced by carefully turning off all lights and appliances, when they are not actually being used. Heat can be turned down an hour before bedtime. Water heater temperature should be maintained near to the temperature desired for use rather than keeping temperatures high and then cooling bath water before use.

Maintaining a large tank of water at a high temperature results in higher losses.

These are all ways expenses for necessary items can be reduced. Others should be eliminated altogether. Families under financial pressure should carefully evaluate whether a second car is actually needed. Second cars eat sizable hunks of a family's income. For example, a U.S. Department of Transportation study in 1982 showed that . . .

> . . . driving even a six to eight year old vehicle as a second car costs $200 to $250 per month when depreciation, maintenance, repairs, tires, gasoline, insurance, taxes and licenses, etc. are all figured in. Costs in owning newer cars can average $350 to $400 per month.[3]

A big portion of this expense can be saved even if the wife and mother uses taxis for emergencies. By careful planning, a wife and mother can have use of a car once or twice a week if the father can use public transportation or participate in a car pool.

Elimination of credit buying produces sizable savings. If a family only has installment debts of $8000 (for a car, boat, camper, furniture, appliances, TV and stereo and charge card balances for gasoline, restaurant charges, clothing purchases, vacation expenses, etc.), the monthly interest charges and debt service fees and costs can total up to $150 per month. Interest will be proportionately higher or lower depending on the debt total.

WHAT DOES A WORKING MOTHER COST A FAMILY?

Mounting financial pressures cause many women to attempt to handle two full-time jobs. To the full-time roles of wife and mother, millions of women have added jobs in offices, factories, restaurants, stores, hospitals, and schools.

Tragically, however, a wife's going to work usually does not solve a family's financial problems. It may actually worsen them. This statement may not seem logical—but it is so. In addition to possibly increasing the financial problems, a wife's leaving the home to work can be the first in a series of steps which result in a broken home and divorce.

In building a happy, stable, Bible-based home in which

both partners fulfill their God-ordained roles, a family
needs to ask . . .

. . . could mother help more by staying at home?

To help find an answer to that question, I will share some
personal history. When my wife and I were married over
thirty years ago, I was a PFC in the Air Force. We had a
total monthly income of $158 a month (including allot-
ments, rations, etc.) Even so, my wife quit her job as a child
welfare worker and has not worked since (at an out-of-the-
home job for wages).

> Each of us had reasons why she did not work even though
> almost all of the other Air Force wives did. She was old-
> fashioned enough to believe that when she got married, that
> her husband was supposed to support her. With this challenge
> to evaluate whether a wife really should work, I quickly came to
> see that all that glitters is not gold.

A working wife can actually cost a family money in the
long run. Additionally, the cost can involve things which
are more important than money.

> Look at some of the direct financial costs when a wife works. In
> the average family tax bracket, between one-quarter and one-
> third of the wife's salary is withheld for Social Security and
> state and federal income taxes. If she works in an office or
> store, she needs to look her best. This requires extra clothes and
> perhaps more frequent trips to the beauty parlor. Both cost
> money. In other kinds of work, the extra expense maybe for
> uniforms or union dues.

> There are transportation expenses. When a wife works a
> second car often becomes necessary. (With my wife not working
> we were married for fourteen years before becoming a two-car
> family). Even an old second car can take one-fifth to one-
> quarter of a wife's take home pay when costs of the car,
> insurance, gas and oil, and repairs and maintenance costs are
> figured (see page 199).

> When the wife works, a family eats out a lot more. Higher
> priced convenience foods are used more often when a family eats
> at home. With the wife working there often is not time to plan
> and carefully prepare economical, top quality, tasty meals.

Because of such expenses, a successful engineer became
rather upset recently. He came to realize that his family
nets only $6,000 out of his wife's $16,000-a-year job as a

public school teacher. When there are children, babysitting costs eat up another $85 to $250 a month of the "extra" income. If this is true with a $16,000 income what is the net when the entire second income only totals $6,000? In some cases, the family's real financial picture may actually deteriorate when the wife goes to work

There are indirect costs as well when a wife works. The prospect of a second income (which actually may be very small) is often the excuse for loosening purse strings and splurging. The standard of living seems to jump (at least its cost does) and soon the family cannot get along without the second income.

The intangible costs can be even more important. A working mother comes home tense and tired to face all the responsibilities of a homemaker. When the essentials are done, there is very little time left to be a mother and a wife. Children come home from school to an empty house, a TV set, or a babysitter. They get lots of packaged food, thrown together meals and evenings out at a fast food restaurant. Working mothers have too little time to talk to their children, read to them, teach them Bible, or to lovingly supervise their schoolwork. Many children grow up in a family all alone.

Church attendance suffers. "It's our only real day off, you know." Because of rotating schedules, some husbands and wives who work rarely share a day off.

The working wife develops a sense of independence. She earns her own money. She thinks she should be able to spend it. The husband's ego is marred now that he is no longer the real provider. Often a job can be the first step toward breaking up the home.

Children suffer. Children need mothers who are full-time homemakers. The "experts" are finally discovering that children who grow up in day care situations suffer throughout life.

In the late 1970's, best selling author, Selma Fraiberg, was one of the first to raise serious questions about the effects of day-care upbringing on children. In her book, *Every Child's Birthright: In Defense of Mothering*[4], she strongly advocates the case for full-time mothers. Surveying the damage to children who have spent 10 to 12 hours daily in day care, she writes:

Children who have been deprived of mothering, and who have formed no personal human bonds during the first two years of life, show permanent impairment of the capacity to make human attachments in later childhood....The degree of impairment is roughly equal to the degree of deprivation.

She further explains the dangers, saying:

The "unattached" child not only experiences difficulty in forming any subsequent relationship, but his intellectual functions are impaired during the first eighteen months of life. Specifically, conceptual thinking remains depressed even when favorable environmental conditions are provided in the second and third years. In the area of aggression, these children reveal serious disorders of impulse control.

When the day-care center is a mother-substitute during much of the day, Selma Fraiberg concludes:

We do not need to "prove" that such programs can be damaging to many children. When a child spends eleven to twelve hours of his waking day in the care of indifferent custodians, no parent and no educator can say that the child's development is being promoted or enhanced, and common sense tells us that children are harmed by indifference.

The child who spends most of his waking day in an environment of indifference is a likely candidate for what Fraiberg calls the disease of "non-attachment." It is frequently incurable. In a review of Fraiberg's book, Solveig Eggerz commented that these "non-attached" children....

...grow into the "hollow men" of society, persons who in their most harmless form, wander lonely and indifferent through life, and in the worst instances may be capable of blood-curdling crimes without a prick of conscience. Once a child is several years old, the chances of reversing this development are slim.[5]

Fraiberg says of the children afflicted with the disease of "non-attachment:"

Today we see many of these children in Head Start programs. These are the three and four year olds who seem unaware of other people or things. They are the silent, unsmiling, poor ghosts of children who wander through a brightly painted nursery as if it were a cemetery. Count it a victory if, after six months of work with such a child, you can get him to smile in greeting you or learn your name.

These pitiful, non-attached, non-relating children are

among the most tragic of those diagnosed as learning
disabled when they start to school.

Further refutation of the "benefits" of day-care for
children came during the early 1980's, when a series of
additional studies. . . .

> . . . .suggest there may be more negative results from day-care
> centers than we thought.

That was the conclusion of University of North Carolina
Professor Dale Farran in a study based on about one-
hundred children in Chapel Hill, North Carolina. She
found that those who attended day-care centers from
infancy through age five were "fifteen times as aggressive
as those who did not spend their early years in day-care."
Both physical and verbal attacks on other children were
much more common among children raised in day cares.

In an article on day care in the September 1982 *Parents'*
magazine, Professor Farran said children from day care
centers are. . .

> . . . .more active (hyper), more easily frustrated, less cooperative
> with adults, more oriented to children than adults, more
> distractible and less task oriented.

Professor Farran's findings will be disputed by other
"experts." However, there are trends no one can deny.
During the twenty years when day care has become a major
industry and mothers have moved en masse into the work
force, children's problems have snowballed. Learning
disabilities have multiplied. Senseless crimes of juvenile
violence against people and property are a scandal. Drug
and alcohol use among teen-agers has soared. Sexual
promiscuity, illegitimate births, abortions, and venereal
disease among the young have reached epidemic propor-
tions. These are some of the awful costs of the mounting
financial pressures which drive mothers out of the home.*

----

*If it is believed that a mother must work outside the home, an
alternative to day-care must be found. If regular, consistent in-the-home
supervision by a caring, dependable older relative is not possible, care in
a private home supervised by a competent, caring mother may be
considered. Ideally, not more than 3 or 4 children (of varying ages)
should be in the home so that each one has the opportunity to develop as
an individual. Extreme care is necessary in selecting this one person
who will care for your child on a regular basis. Many of the child's basic

In addition to these dramatic examples the latest U.S. Department of Education study[4] reveals that children whose mothers work score consistently lower on school achievement tests.

Young people of this troubled day-care generation are now starting their own marriages. They have never had the example of a home in which the husband and wife really fulfill their God-given roles. Many will duplicate the problems and misery their parents experience.

So, what does a working wife actually cost a family? A sober evaluation shows that rather than solving financial problems, the woman's absence from the home can actually create more problems. The true cost in money and quality of life can be tragic. Family relationships can be subjected to unbearable pressures as well.**

GIVE GOD FIRST PLACE

The pathway to financial freedom includes cutting both unnecessary expenses and costs of essentials. Credit buying must be stopped. None of these programs can be effective, however, unless a family starts giving God first place. To give God first place in money matters, He must be given first place in everything.

In the Sermon on the Mount, the Lord Jesus told His disciples:

> Take no thought for your life, what ye shall eat, or what ye shall drink; nor yet for your body, what ye shall put on. Is not the life more than meat, and the body than raiment? (Matthew 6:25).

If we are God's children and His servants, God has a twofold responsibility to provide for our needs. The Lord Jesus promised freedom from financial worries if we assume our place as servants and as children and let the

---

values and attitudes for life and how he will talk, eat, and act will be determined by the mother substitute during the preschool years.

**Young couples should not get married until the husband's pay will support them totally. If the young wife continues working for a time after marriage, her total income should be saved—perhaps for a down payment on a home. In buying a home, the wife's income should not be used in gaining loan approval. If these suggestions are violated, all too often the family gets locked into a life style and commitments which force a wife to work even after children are born.

Heavenly Father provide our needs. To do this, Jesus said:

> Seek ye first the kingdom of God, and his righteousness and all these things shall be added unto you (Matthew 6:33).

God promises to provide all of our needs if we will (1) seek to have Him rule our lives and (2) make righteousness (being like Jesus) the goal of our lives. This is a real and glorious promise. If we fail to give Him first place, no amount of self-effort will produce financial freedom. God's people, the Jews, learned this sad lesson 2500 years ago.

After seventy years in captivity in Babylon, Israel returned to Jerusalem. The foundation was laid for rebuilding the temple. Then the work was set aside. People decided that they first needed to build better homes for themselves. However, nothing worked out right. In words that could have been written for today, the prophet Haggai said:

> Thus saith the Lord of hosts, saying, This people say, The time is not come, the time that the Lord's house should be built.
>
> Then came the word of the Lord by Haggai the prophet, saying, Is it time for you, O ye, to dwell in your cieled houses, and this house [God's] lie waste?
>
> Now therefore thus saith the Lord of hosts; Consider your ways. Ye have sown much, and bring in little; ye eat, but ye have not enough; ye drink, but ye are not filled with drink; ye clothe you, but there is none warm; and he that earneth wages earneth wages to put it into a bag with holes. Thus saith the Lord of hosts; Consider your ways (Haggai 1:2-7).

God will not take second place in any life or home. If your family has been among the many which. . ."eat, but have not enough, drink but are not filled with drink, put on clothes but are not warm, and earn wages to put into a bag with holes," the Lord says:

. . .Consider your ways.

To build a stable home which is satisfying and solvent, it is necessary to put God first, applying His principles to the decisions of life. The Book of Proverbs promises:

> The Lord will not suffer the soul of the righteous to famish: but he casteth away the substance of the wicked. He becometh poor that dealeth with a slack hand: but the hand of the diligent maketh rich. He that gathereth in summer is a wise son: but he

that sleepeth in harvest is a son that causeth shame (Proverbs 10:3-5).

TELL OTHERS

Are you ready to trust the Lord with your finances? Are you ready to start doing things the way God wants? Make the "now and forever" decisions right now to start tithing, stop credit buying, and to eliminate all debt as soon as possible. Then begin to apply suggestions for cutting expenses. Seriously evaluate what a working wife and mother costs your family. Actually, it is impossible to trust God just for finances. He must be trusted in every area of life.

Once your decisions have been made, you need to tell someone. You might share with someone in your family the steps you are taking. It might also be appropriate to share your decisions with your pastor and folks in your church. Trusting God is important. The Bible says that God has great things stored up for those who trust Him. Telling others is the way to see the great things God has stored up released and made real in your life. Psalm 31:19 says:

> Oh how great is thy goodness, which thou hast laid up for them that fear thee; which thou hast wrought [worked out] for them that trust in thee before the sons of men!

Make your decisions. Then tell others and see how God works miracles.

START A SYSTEMATIC SAVINGS PROGRAM

Just getting out of debt should not be the family's only goal. A systematic savings program must be instituted. Savings should be accumulated for several purposes. Cash must be accumulated to pay for things previously financed through credit buying such as cars, vacations, home remodeling and repair, etc. Separate longer-range savings plans need to be established for children's education and for eventual retirement. Avoid insurance which builds up cash equity. It is not a good savings investment on a long-range basis. With inflation a fact of national life, fixed-dollar savings programs for long-range needs are probably not wise. Term-type insurance can be purchased at much lower cost to provide needed protection. The Scriptural basis for saving for the future is found in Proberbs 6:6-11:

> Go to the ant, thou sluggard; consider her ways, and be wise:
> Which having no guide, overseer, or ruler, Provideth her meat
> in the summer, and gathereth her food in the harvest. How long
> wilt thou sleep, O sluggard? when wilt thou arise out of thy
> sleep? Yet a little sleep, a little slumber, a little folding of the
> hands to sleep: So shall thy poverty come as one that travelleth,
> and thy want as an armed man.

CHAPTER XIII

1. St. Louis *Globe Democrat*, Aug. 17, 1981
2. Ibid., Mar. 15, 1983
3. St. Louis *Post Dispatch*, Nov. 9, 1982
4. Fraiberg, *Every Child's Birthright: In Defense of Mothering*, Basic Books, New York, 1977, quoted in *Human Events*, May 20, 1978.
5. *Human Events*, May 20, 1978
6. St. Louis *Globe Democrat*, Jun 27, 1983

Chapter XIV

DON'T STOP!

> *...continue thou in the things which thou hast learned and hast been assured of...And let us not be weary in well doing for in due season we shall reap, if we faint not.*
>
> *--II Timothy 3:14--Galatians 6:9*

CHILD RAISING EXPERTS quoted in the first chapter stress the importance of the first three years. They are vitally important. If a good foundation is not laid in the early years, children will bear some of the consequences no matter how much remedial work is done later. By the same token, parents cannot quit home training and character building once children get a good start in school---even if they go to a good Christian school

If you will faithfully follow the suggestions in this book, a number of things will happen. Your child will receive a solid foundation for school and life. You will work to make your own life a good model for your children to follow. Your child will develop a real sense of security as you and your partner build a stable, secure, satisfying marriage and home. As you provide for the child's needs, stimulate his interest in the surrounding world, and develop his or her character you will build a close personal relationship.

The child training process should never stop. The challenges are different when the baby becomes three or six or twelve or eighteen years old, but there still will be challenges. There are opportunities at every age as well. If you do your job well, you will build relationships with your children so they will be willing and anxious to have your help and advice and encouragement when they start raising your grandchildren!

Your life and example and the training you give to your

children will affect them *and many future generations.*
That truth is illustrated by the findings of researchers who
studied two families who lived in New York state in the 18th
and 19th centuries. The different lifestyles of these two
families dramatically affected their children for five or six
generations. In 1874, R.A. Dugdale, a researcher for the
New York State Penal Association, studied the longterm
record of a family called "Jukes" in his report. Dugdale
found:

> Max Jukes and his brother married sisters. They did not
> believe in Christian training. They had 1,026 descendants.
> Three hundred of them died when very young. Many others
> had poor health. At least 140 of them served time in the
> penitentiary for an average of 13 years each; 190 were public
> prostitutes; and there were 100 drunkards in the group.

Over a hundred-year period, Dugdale estimated that the
family cost New York state $1,200,000. With inflation and
more liberal welfare programs today, these two families
and their descendants could easily cost taxpayers hundreds
of millions of dollars. Contrast the misery experienced and
caused by the Jukes family with another record:

> Jonathan Edwards became a Christian and married a girl of
> like belief. After graduating from Yale in 1720, he became a
> preacher. From their union, he and his wife had 729 descen-
> dants. Among them were 300 preachers, 65 college professors,
> 13 university presidents, 60 authors, 3 congressman, and a vice
> president of the United States. Except for Aaron Burr, a
> grandson of Edwards who married a girl of questionable
> character, the family did not cost the state a single dollar.

The marked difference between the two families is the
result of true heart conversions and the home life and
training of the children. Five or six generations were
affected. The contrast illustrates the teaching of the Word
of God which says:

> Blessed is the man that feareth the Lord, that delighteth
> greatly in his commandments. His seed [children and grand-
> children] shall be mighty upon the earth: the generation of the
> upright shall be blessed (Psalm 112:1-2).

So what ever your children's ages right now, start
training. Then do not ever stop! Teach them and train

them. Then re-inforce the training by requiring them to
keep on doing what they have been taught and trained to
do. It is a lifelong process!

As you start and as you continue, keep in mind this
concise yet very wise plan for rearing children. It was given
by an anonymous caller to an open line radio program. She
said:

> Love your children. Then train them to live and act in such a
> way that others will love them too.

To do this exciting and rewarding job will require more
than just one reading of this book. After your husband or
wife has read it also, read it through together. Discuss it
section by section. Start applying the lessons and principles
to the needs of your child. Periodically reread the entire
book or a pertinent section to gain additional insights as
you grow personally. Use it as a means of taking inventory.
Most of all, just start "doing." You will never be a perfect
parent. No one is, but do the best you can and remember
that love covers a multitude of shortcomings.

If you get off the track, God will show you. In the
meantime, what you have already seen you need to do, just
start doing it!

That's the key to growing as a Christian. It is also the
secret to becoming the parent your child needs. Get to it---
and DON'T EVER STOP!

OTHER HELPFUL CHILD-REARING BOOKS

(To order, use form on page 214)

IF I COULD CHANGE MY MOM AND DAD $3.50

Compiled from letters written by children (ages 5 to 17) to the author who is a Christian youth worker. The book gives valuable insights into how children see and feel about their parents in ten vital areas.

RAISING A BRIGHTER CHILD IN
10 MINUTES A DAY $7.95

Many ideas for lessons to be taught in daily "mini-school" sessions for children starting at age 2 or earlier and continuing even after school starts.

HONEY FOR A CHILD'S HEART $6.95

A heart-warming guide for using reading together as a family to build character, personal relationships and an interest in reading in children.

THE MAKING OF GEORGE WASHINGTON $1.95

A well-researched and very readable account of how George Washington was trained as a boy by his parents.

HOW TO REAR INFANTS $5.50
HOW TO REAR CHILDREN $5.50
HOW TO REAR TEEN-AGERS $5.50

These three books by Dr. Jack Hyles, pastor of America's largest Sunday school, have been a help and blessing to hundreds of thousands of parents.

HELPFUL BOOKS FOR CHRISTIAN GROWTH

(To order, use form on page 214)

WHAT CHRISTIANS BELIEVE $2.95

An easy-to-understand Bible-based guide to basic Christian doctrine and conduct. An ideal help for new believers.

WHAT'S A GIRL TO DO? $1.00

A readable, interesting guide to dating and future marriage by Louisa Brown. Mrs. Brown's book gives teen-agers important helps in preparing for dating and ultimate marriage. Helpful also for young mothers who may have missed some of these foundational concepts when growing up. Very interesting reading.

THE PRINCIPLES OF SPIRITUAL GROWTH $1.95

Christians grow the same way they get saved:
They see their need, learn what Christ did to meet
the need, believe that what Christ has done meets
need, and then experience the actual fulfillment of
the need. This little book gives the plan and the
principles for making it real.

THE BLOOD OF JESUS $1.00

The touching story of a man who came to realize
that although he prayed, attended church, and
taught Sunday school that he did not know God
personally. His personal story plus twelve short
messages on why the Lord Jesus has to shed His
blood has sold millions of copies during the last
120 years.

THE HOLY BIBLE $3.50

The King James Version of the Bible is the most
accurate and beautiful English translation of the
Old and New Testaments. It has been read and
loved by more Christians of all denominations
than any other since 1611.

OTHER BOOKS BY JOHN STORMER

(To order, use form on page 214)

NONE DARE CALL IT TREASON $3.95

A 7-million copy best-seller since published in
1964. John Stormer's first book traces the growth
of world communism and the simultaneous decay
in America's churches, schools, press, unions, and
political organizations which have produced "The
Revolution We've Lived Through."

THE DEATH OF A NATION $3.95

John Stormer's second book spotlights how the
United States is destroying itself by fighting its
enemies, including communism, worldwide with
one hand while aiding the same enemies with the
other hand.

ORDER FORM

CHILD-REARING BOOKS

- [ ] If I Could Change My Mom and Dad . . . . $ 3.50
- [ ] Raising A Brighter Child In Ten-Minutes A Day . . . 7.95
- [ ] Honey For A Child's Heart 6.95
- [ ] The Making Of George Washington 1.95
- [ ] How To Rear Infants 5.50
- [ ] How To Rear Children 5.50
- [ ] How To Rear Teen-Agers 5.50

BOOKS FOR CHRISTIAN GROWTH

- [ ] What Christians Believe . . . . $ 2.95
- [ ] What's A Girl To Do? 1.00
- [ ] The Blood Of Jesus 1.00
- [ ] The Holy Bible-King James Version 3.50
- [ ] Principles of Spiritual Growth 1.95

BOOKS BY JOHN STORMER

- [ ] None Dare Call It Treason . . . . $ 3.95
- [ ] The Death of a Nation 3.95

Total for Books Ordered: $_____

For shipping and handling,
add $1.00 for the first book and
$.50 for each additional one: $_____

Missouri residents add 5½% sales tax: $_____

Total: $_____

LIBERTY BELL PRESS
P.O. Box 32, Florissant, MO 63032

Enclosed find $_____ to cover cost of the books checked on the
above list. Send to:

Name_____

Street _____

City_____ State_____ Zip_____

Liberty Bell Press,

P. O. Box 32, Florissant, MO, 63032

Send me _____ copies of **Growing Up God's Way.**

Payment of $ _____ is enclosed (send check or money order.)

Missouri residents add 5 1/2 % sales tax.

Name _____

Street _____

City and State _____ Zip Code _____

HELP
NEW
PARENTS

Give GROWING UP GOD'S WAY

To Friends, Relatives, Neighbors,
The People in Your Church or School,
And All New Parents in Your Area.

Thousands of copies have already been distributed in every part of the United States. Churches are distributing the book to the parents of all new babies born in the areas they serve. Businessmen who recognize that people of character are good employees and good customers are distributing them to customers, friends, etc. Individuals are distributing them to young married couples, giving them to all families in their church or school, mailing them to people listed in new birth lists, etc.

Do your part. Order copies of *Growing Up God's Way* now at the low quantity prices below.

Order Form on Page 215

QUANTITY PRICES

1 copy:	$3.95	10 copies:	$15	100 copies:	$90
5 copies	$10.00	25 copies:	$30	500 copies:	$350

1000 or more copies: $.60 each

LIBERTY BELL PRESS

P. O. Box 32   Florissant, MO 63032